NATIVE HARVESTS

HARVESTS

Recipes and Botanicals
of the American Indian

BARRIE KAVASCH

*The purchase of this book benefits the American Indian Archaeological Institute
and continues an Education and Ethnobotany Endowment*

Grateful acknowledgment is made to the following for permission to reprint
previously published material:

Ballantine Books, A Division of Random House, Inc.: Excerpt from *Eating from the
Wild* by Dr. Anne Marie Stewart. Copyright © 1975 by Dr. Anne Marie Stewart
and Leon Kronoff.

Doubleday and Co., Inc. and McIntosh and Otis, Inc.: Excerpt from *The Art of
American Indian Cooking* by Yeffe Kimball and Jean Anderson. Copyright © 1965
by Yeffe Kimball and Jean Anderson. Reprinted by permission of Doubleday
and Co., Inc. and McIntosh and Otis, Inc.

National Geographic Society: Excerpt from "Mexico's Window on the Past,"
National Geographic Magazine, October, 1968.

Stackpole Books: Excerpt from *Feasting Free on Wild Edibles* by Bradford Angier.
Copyright © 1966 by Stackpole Books.

Walker and Company: Excerpt from *A Cooking Legacy* by Virginia T. Elverson and
Mary Ann McLanahan. Copyright © 1975 by Virginia Elverson and Mary Ann
McLanahan. Used with permission of the publisher, Walker and Company.

Library of Congress Cataloging in Publication Data
Kavasch, Barrie.
Native harvests.
Bibliography: p.
Includes index.
1. Indians of North America — Food.   2. Ethnobotany
— North America.   3. Cookery, Indian.   I. Title.
E98.F7K38   1979   641.5   78-21791
ISBN 0-394-50411-9
9   8   7   6   5   4   3   2

To the American Indians
their history
and
their future
and
to the American Indian
Archaeological Institute

SONGS OF HUEXOTZINGO
(Aztec Poetic Lament)

Will I leave only this:
Like the flowers that wither?
Will nothing last in my name —
Nothing of my fame here on earth?

At least flowers!
At least song!

FOREWORD

The first edition of *Native Harvests* was prepared by the author under the auspices of the American Indian Archaeological Institute, in Washington, Connecticut. The AIAI is a unique regional resource center for education and research in New England. The center is designed to answer three major needs:

1. to discover and disseminate American Indian prehistory in New England before it is lost forever
2. to provide invaluable services, staff, and facilities that would not duplicate, nor have to be duplicated by other professional archaeological, historical, educational, or research institutions
3. to provide a strong link between the large multidisciplinary education and research institutions and the small-town or regional historical and archaeological societies

The center is located on fifteen acres of wooded land adjoining a 1,500-acre park along the banks of the beautiful Shepaug River and thus furnishes an ideal as well as a practical setting for such an institution. Facilities consist of class, seminar, and work rooms; educational and research libraries; an exhibit hall; a research room; and a Habitat Trail, which meanders through the natural woodlands surrounding the center. The Habitat Trail represents the major environments Indian people experienced in New England over the past ten thousand years.

First opened on July 1, 1975, the AIAI is a nonprofit educational institution that depends for financial support upon memberships, donations, visitations, and modest charges for educational and research programs.

The meteoric growth of the institute since its inception is mute testimony to the deep and total commitment of a rapidly growing number of people not only in New England but over the entire United States. We have an opportunity in this generation that may never arise again. We are participating in the discovery and preservation of over ten thousand years of a valuable and irreplaceable human cultural history, that of the American Indian of New England. Moreover, we know that time is running out. The last remaining sites that contain these secrets will soon be destroyed forever by the "progress" of our own civilization.

How can we put a price on this history? These people, our forebears and predecessors here in New England, lived where we do now and surely learned much over countless centuries about this land. Their history offers modern man not only a potentially viable model of an alternative life-style but also many hitherto unknown facts about our environment, including a whole host of practical and often extremely beneficial uses of our native plants. It is with great pleasure — and great humility — that we of the American Indian Archaeological Institute are able to share with Barrie Kavasch, the talented author of *Native Harvests*, a small part of the precious legacy of our New England Indians. And, because of our shared concern for this extraordinarily important aspect of our research, all funds received by the American Indian Archaeological Institute for the sale of this publication will go into a permanent ethnobotanical endowment fund to ensure the perpetuation of this project.

Let it not be said that modern man, in his rush to meet the stars, had neither the time nor the inclination to learn his own history . . . lying buried beneath his feet.

EDMUND K. SWIGART
President
American Indian Archaeological Institute
Washington, Connecticut

PERSONAL
ACKNOWLEDGMENTS

An author's greatest privilege is to be given the chance to expand her first book, especially with the publisher's enthusiastic support. I am deeply grateful to my editors, Anne Freedgood, Betsy Amster, and Susan Payne, and to the book's designer, Elissa Ichiyasu. This is the best team I know of!

I'd also like to thank Dr. Stephen K-M. Tim, taxonomist at the Brooklyn Botanic Garden, whose comments on the manuscript were extremely helpful.

Along with three new chapters, many new recipes of ancestral origins are included in this enlarged edition of *Native Harvests*. The chapters on ferns, lichens and mosses, wild mushrooms, and poisonous plants amplify still further the ethnobotany of our first Americans. I have also added as many new botanicals as research permitted, along with as many new illustrations as I could accomplish.

A number of our native botanicals are common not only across the United States but also worldwide. Long before the twentieth century, many botanicals (like the birds) were globe-trotters. The primary emphasis of *Native Harvests* is on the wealth of native flora, but it also encompasses numerous introduced species with significant usages by the Amerindians. To indicate the exchange and sharing between cultures — Old World and New World — has been one of the primary aims of my research. No longer regional to New England alone, this expanded edition studies the panorama of Amerindian influences on our food and lifeways.

With ethnobotany the center of my attention, I have expanded the number of wild (and cultivated) botanicals included in this book. Because they have been drawn together from so many different sources, I have reviewed and correlated the wild vascular plants with Gray's *Manual of Botany*, eighth edition, and the cultivated plants with *Hortus Third*. The additional reference and guide books used are listed in the bibliography. The plant taxonomy is a useful tool, but certainly secondary to the use and understanding of *Native Harvests*. With *caution, moderation*, and *correct identification* paramount, I again invite you to enjoy the wild harvests.

BARRIE KAVASCH
Bridgewater, Connecticut

CONTENTS

INTRODUCTION

Food was woven more intimately into the fabric of daily life in ancient times than it is today. It directly fueled physical accomplishments, and almost all work of aboriginal peoples was done by their own power. Long before the native Americans established seasonal settlements, planted and harvested crops, and domesticated animals, they had accumulated an extensive knowledge of plant usage and food preparation. Through observation of their natural environment and experimentation they knew the botanicals to use for foods, medicines, and cosmetics, and which botanicals satisfied the other necessities of clothing, shelter, cordage, and tools. After settling into early horticultural bands, groups, and societies, the Indians continued to use and learn more about the multitudes of wild plants.

A stable culture depends upon a stable food supply. The dawn of farming evolved with the needs of the aboriginal cultures — thousands of years ago. Many of our common cultigens — or cultivated plants — were developed from wild plants by three great Indian nations of South and Meso-America: the Incas of Peru, who irrigated and terraced their South American fields; the Mayas of Central America, who farmed in the fertile wet jungles; and the Aztecs of Mexico, who cleared and burned their arid fields. Numerous North American tribes also cultivated, to some extent, the various wild botanicals that best proliferated in their floral environment.

With experimental ingenuity, these sophisticated early cultures domesticated and hybridized over 150 botanicals, including 6 species of corn (over 150 varieties and colors); 5 main species of beans (with countless colored varieties); squash, gourds, and pumpkins; tomatoes; peppers; peanuts; strawberries; blueberries; Jerusalem artichokes; potatoes, both white and sweet; chocolate; vanilla; sunflowers; and many others.

Squash, gourds, and pumpkins are believed to be the first plants cultivated by these early peoples, over eight thousand years ago, while corn was first cultivated (probably from a wild highland grass) over seven thousand years ago, and beans over four thousand years ago.

Aside from Indian horticultural achievements, there were freshwater and saltwater foods, game, and thousands of varieties of edible wild plants, seasonally available, to be enjoyed raw or cooked. The most important and widely used foods we know today are of native American origin. Almost 75 percent of our present food plants were new to Europeans five hundred years ago. Captain John Smith, writing in 1607, noted that the settlers of Jamestown, Virginia, would have starved if the Indians of that region had not brought corn, squash, and beans to them. This famous Indian triad, the "three sisters," soon became the most important foods in pioneer America. Their planting, harvesting, and preparation reflected the myriad native American usages and customs.

Colonial American pioneers left diaries and journals telling tragic stories of the deaths of nine out of every ten early settlers. "Starving time" it was called. The forests teemed with game, large and small; the waters swarmed with fish; fruits and vegetables were plentiful. Unfortunately many of these early Colonials were city-bred and unfamiliar with country living; even those from rural backgrounds were unprepared for wilderness existence. They failed to bring the necessary tools and equipment and knowledge to cope with their new way of life, so their spiritual diet became one of fear and desperation.

Adaptation was the key to survival. The American Indian became both teacher and savior, instructing the settlers in hunting, food preparation and preservation. Cookbooks from home would have been of little use to the often illiterate housewife, who found herself obliged to prepare ingredients unknown to her in England or Holland, such as corn, pumpkin, and squash.*

*Virginia T. Elverson and Mary Ann McLanahan, A Cooking Legacy (New York: Walker & Co., 1975), p. 1.

The Eastern Woodlands Indians were creative and accomplished cooks. Before extensive horticulture, their varied diets were gleaned from the land, lakes, marshes, and coastal regions, and the earth was both their storage cellar and their oven. Early colonial writings describe settlers finding "aboriginal barnes" (underground storage pits lined and covered with tree bark) from Cape Cod north and south through the Virginias. These "windfalls" reflected the prosperity of a gathering and harvesting people, who had put by their surpluses against the winter.

Native American cuisine is a continental cooking entirely our own. The basis of what has become most classic is uniquely American Indian: barbeques and clambakes, steamed lobsters and stuffed oysters, clam and corn chowders and gumbos, multitudes of cranberry creations, Boston baked beans, Brunswick stew, mincemeat pie and spoonbread, plus the infinite variety of cornbreads and puddings and dumplings — dishes as unusual as they are delicious, reflecting as they do the various styles of so many Indian cultures. The cultural differences, linked to distinct geographical locations and regional growing seasons, determined how these various peoples lived, what they ate, and how they cooked.

> American Indians never were a unit. They were scattered in hundreds of tribes with hundreds of cultures and customs. It is these tribal variations that have given color and character to the American past, and a wondrously wide variety of dishes to the American diet.*

Native Harvests reflects the native usage of wild and cultivated botanicals, both indigenous and introduced species. In keeping with the style of food preparation five hundred to one thousand years ago in North America, the recipes collected here should be used merely as springboards, guides to tastier, more creative cooking. As a body of recipes they are salt-free, principally because salt was not a widely used or natural food substance in the early American diet, except for its occasional use during coastal festivities and in a few inland areas.

According to personal taste preference, you may add salt and pepper and your favorite seasonings, or you may remain with the natural "earth seasonings." In those recipes that call for a particularly unusual ingredient I have suggested substitutions whenever possible. In general, flours may usually be substituted for one another. Because corn contains only a

*Will Rogers, Jr., Foreword to *The Art of American Indian Cooking*, by Yeffe Kimball and Jean Anderson (Garden City, N.Y.: Doubleday & Co., Inc., 1965).

small amount of gluten, it may be blended with other flours, especially wheat or rye, in order to lighten breadlike preparations. However, keep in mind that most Indian breads were relatively heavy, sturdy creations. Also, unprocessed peanut butter — the kind available at health food stores and at some commercial supermarkets — may be substituted for the various nut butters many of the recipes call for. Similarly, it is possible in these recipes to substitute one berry for another if necessary, or to use raisins or currants when berries are out of season.

Although a good deal of botanical information is included in this book, *Native Harvests* is intended to serve more as a cookbook than a botanical guide. I have profiled or illustrated most of the plants used in the recipes, but plants familiar to everybody — garden-variety potatoes, tomatoes, corn, and beans, for example — have not received the same treatment. To make the best and the safest use of *Native Harvests*, all foraging and gathering of "the edible wild" should be done in conjunction with dependable trail or identification guides. Consult the reference guide at the back of this book, your library, or a local bookshop for suggestions.

Taste the native harvests. Eat sparingly until you cultivate your new taste experiences. Identify carefully; avoid mistakes. Only a very small proportion of the plant kingdom is poisonous: Less than 1 percent of the known 500,000 plant species are truly deadly (see chapter 13, "Poisonous Wild Plants," for more information). Know your food sources, and take only the plant parts you need. Most important, never overharvest a limited area. Enjoy the integration of wild and cultivated foods for better nutrition. There are so many variables in nature. You have to exercise your own unique "earth sense" in developing seasonings, as well as recipes, to suit your own tastes.

NATIVE HARVESTS

I

NATURE'S SEASONINGS

Wild seasonings are as fascinating and limitless as the great outdoors. A knowledge of the safe versus the toxic is vital and easy to acquire. The early Americans evolved an extensive usage of seasonal, indigenous North American flavorings, which is impressive and beneficial to us today.

Use herbs and spices sparingly to enhance, not dominate, the natural flavors of foods. As a rule, a recipe to serve 6 people can use $1/2$ teaspoon (or less) of any coarsely chopped dried herb or spice. Dried herbs are used in less quantity because of their more concentrated form and stronger flavors. Add most herbs during the last 5 to 10 minutes of cooking time, or they will become bitter and lose their nutritive value. The best aroma and flavor of herbs, spices, seeds, and nuts is contained in their aromatic oils, which dissipate with time, some lasting much longer than others. Leaf herbs have the most aromatic oil and the best flavor when fresh.

Early Americans also knew the special properties of *ashes* mixed with their foods, or in water, for various preparations. Ashes of distinctive woods such as cedar, juniper, hickory, and so on, were definite flavorings, as well as cleansing and digestive agents. Ashes also bleach and soften some foods and add trace minerals, subtly influencing taste and consistency. Ashes in water create lye, which will harden and chemically change the substances to which it is added.

Spoon fresh ashes out of a fireplace, woodburning stove, or campfire for use in the recipes. (In some cases substitutions are indicated.) Be sure not to scrape the ashes out of the fireplace, or you will pick up unwanted and harmful tars and residues.

Nuts and Seeds

Nut and seed butters and oils were the primary nutritive seasoning among most native Americans. They provided the greatest flavor accents and were a widely used staple in native diets.

Botanically speaking, nuts are any hard-shelled fruit with a large food store, whereas seeds are smaller and have more limited food reserves; both will keep more or less indefinitely.

Nuts were used extensively by many American Indian tribes who taught the early colonists how to gather and prepare them for flour, pastes, oil, butter, pottages and dyes. Part of the Indian's annual cycle of activities included the autumn harvest of the black walnuts, acorns, hickory nuts and chestnuts. Nuts were an important item in the Indian's diet and as winter progressed and the food supply became low, they depended more and more upon them for nourishment. They deemed nuts so important that several tribes named their moons or times of the year after them. For example, the Natchez Indians called their twelfth moon (around the latter part of January) that of the Chestnut and the thirteenth moon (February) that of the nuts.*

BEECHNUTS (*Fagus grandifolia*) are one of the most flavorful products of our northern forests. They are best gathered in late October or November after heavy frosts have dropped them to the ground. Delicious raw or cooked, beechnuts are best gathered before dawn, when possible, to beat the squirrels. Roasted beechnuts, when ground, can be used as a fine caffeine-free coffee. Approximately one sixth of the nut's weight is oil, which is easily extracted by mashing and pressing the small nuts into a paste or by boiling and skimming the oil off the surface of the cooled broth. The flavor of this oil improves with time and keeps well. Beechnuts can also be made into a nutritious *flour* by simply mashing or grinding the nuts and allowing the paste to dry out completely; then grind further, depending on the fineness desired.

*Dr. Anne Marie Stewart and Leon Kronoff, *Eating from the Wild* (New York: Ballantine Books, 1975), p. 239.

Beech trees were an important part of the Iroquois diet. The inner bark (like that of the pine) was dried, ground, and used to make bread. The young beech leaves were also cooked as greens in the spring.

North American oaks (about 60 native spp.) are divided into two groups: WHITE OAKS *(Quercus alba)* and RED OAKS *(Quercus rubra)*. White oaks generally have rounded lobed leaves and sweet acorns that mature in one season. Red oaks generally have pointed bristle-tipped lobed leaves and bitter acorns that usually require two years to mature.

Oaks of all species produce acorns, which were probably the most important and plentiful nut foot for most tribes. All acorns are edible, nutritious food, but some require careful preparation to make them palatable and safe. White oak acorns may be eaten raw, but before eating

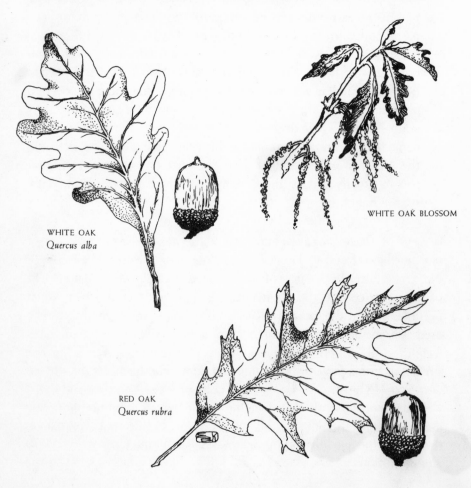

WHITE OAK
Quercus alba

WHITE OAK BLOSSOM

RED OAK
Quercus rubra

red oak acorns it is first essential to leach out the bitter, constipating tannin that makes them toxic. The shelled acorns are soaked in several water baths, sometimes mixed with wood ashes, until the nutmeats sweeten.

Most nutmeats, including sweet white oak acorns, were eaten raw by a number of tribes, especially the Algonquins. Nuts were pounded into meal to be used in breads, soups, and for seasonings; they were also ground in a mortar with water to make a flavorful *nut "milk"* to add to various dishes. *Nut oils* were rendered by boiling the nutmeats and meal, then skimming off the oil. This nutritious staple was used to prepare and to season vegetables, potherbs, and meats, and to spread on breads. The breads were usually "cakes" made by mixing cornmeal with what was left in the bottom of the pot after nut oils were rendered, and then frying this batter in hot fat or roasting it in hot coals.

OIL OF OAK was prepared and used by many Eastern Woodlands tribes. The acorns were pounded into flour and boiled in water containing maple-wood ashes, whereupon the oil was skimmed off. The flour was retained and used in breads and cereals.

HICKORY MILK, a staple ingredient in Creek Indian cooking, was prepared by pounding the shelled dried hickory nuts, then boiling this meal in water and straining and reserving the oily part of the liquid, which was rich, like fresh cream. This was especially well used in their various corn preparations.

HAZELNUTS (*Corylus americana* and *C. cornuta*) are excellent nut meats enjoyed raw when they ripen in late summer and early fall. They are also easily ground into a nutritious flour. The dense hazelnut bush flourishes throughout the northeastern United States, bordering fields, hedgerows, and woods.

BLACK WALNUTS (*Juglans nigra*) and BUTTERNUTS (*Juglans cinerea*) are tall hardwood trees much prized for their wood. They are becoming somewhat scarce in many regions. Both produce delicious nuts, tough to crack but worth the effort. The nut butter can be prepared by smashing the husked nuts and boiling in water until the nutmeats and oils rise to the surface and can be skimmed off, while the shell pieces settle to the bottom of the pot. The oil can then be separated from the meats, which can, in turn, be dried and used as a tasty flour.

AMERICAN CHESTNUT (*Castanea dentata*). The only noted Indian remedy for whooping cough records that the chestnut leaves are steeped, with the resulting tea used as a warm astringent drink. The autumn nuts were a highly valued food crop among northeastern Indians and settlers. Once widespread, the American chestnut has been attacked and almost eradicated from our forests by an Oriental fungus blight, which struck our continent in 1904. Experimental forestry is working to inhibit the deadly fungus, and a few American chestnuts are able to resist the blight with the help of a hypovirulent fungus that seems to be able to combat the initial infection.

The delectable chestnut is one of the most popular nuts to roast. Approximately 11 percent protein and 7 percent fat, it is a nutritious and versatile food source with numerous culinary uses.

SUNFLOWER SEEDS (*Helianthus* spp.) from the native North American annual were used extensively by many tribes. The seeds are an excellent protein source raw or roasted. *Sunflower seed oil* is extracted by bruising and boiling the seeds, then skimming the oily residue off the broth. The ground paste, retaining its natural oil, makes a fine *butter*. The roasted seeds and shells make an interesting coffee drink.

SUNFLOWER SEED CAKES (15 cakes)

3 cups shelled sunflower seeds, fresh or
    dried
3 cups water

6 tablespoons fine cornmeal
2 teaspoons maple syrup
$^{1}/_{2}$ cup oil

Simmer the seeds in the water in a heavy saucepan, covered, for 1 hour. Drain and grind.

Mix the cornmeal and syrup into the ground seeds, 1 tablespoonful at a time, to make a stiff dough. Shape into firm, flat cakes 3 inches in diameter.

Brown the cakes in hot oil in a heavy skillet on both sides. Drain on brown paper and serve hot.

TOASTED PUMPKIN OR SQUASH SEEDS

Spread clean seeds on foil-covered baking sheets. Sprinkle lightly with oil. May be flavored with such herbs as oregano, mint, coltsfoot (for saltiness), and so on. Roast at 325° F until crisp and brown — about 20 minutes. Serve immediately, or cool and store in airtight containers.

NUT BUTTERS AND SEED BUTTERS

Grind 1 cup or more shelled dried nuts or seeds into a paste, using stones, a mortar and pestle, or a blender. Many nut butters (pastes) are sweet enough plain. However, others may require a teaspoon or two of honey or maple syrup mixed in to taste.

This excellent, nutritious topping is great on homemade breads and cakes, or served with fresh fruit, or on fresh, crisp vegetables. Nut and seed butters are very rich and should be used sparingly. Keep refrigerated to retard flavor loss and spoilage.

FLAVORED BUTTERS

SPICE (HERB) BUTTER. To ½ cup nut or seed butter, add 2 tablespoons chopped fresh dillweed (or your favorite herb). Add 1 teaspoon honey and 10 crushed allspice or juniper berries, fresh or dried. Blend together thoroughly and seal in a jar or crock. Keep refrigerated.

MUSTARD BUTTER (for fish and game). To 1 cup sunflower seed butter add 2 tablespoons wild mustard seeds, soaked and crushed in 2 tablespoons corn oil and 1 tablespoon bee pollen. Blend thoroughly and store in a covered jar in the refrigerator.

BEECHNUT-CLOVER BUTTER To 1 cup beechnut butter, add 3 tablespoons dried white clover blossoms and their seeds and 1 tablespoon bee pollen. Blend thoroughly and store. Beechnut butter has the greatest keeping quality of all nut butters. Store in a covered jar in the refrigerator.

MINT BUTTER To ½ cup acorn butter, cream in 2 tablespoons ground fresh mint leaves and 1 teaspoon honey. Store in a covered jar in the refrigerator.

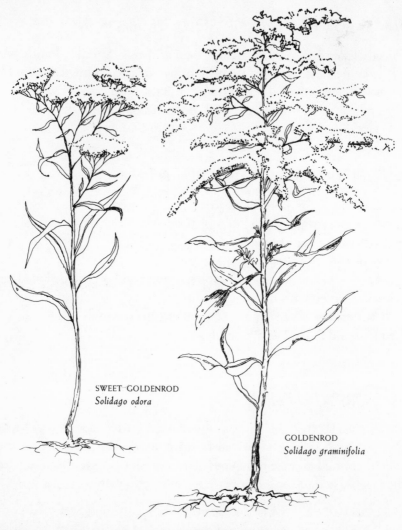

SWEET GOLDENROD
Solidago odora

GOLDENROD
Solidago graminifolia

HICKORY NUT-CORN PUDDING (serves 6)

1 ¹/₂ cups cooked corn
¹/₂ cup shelled dried hickory nuts,
    chopped
2 tablespoons nut butter (see page 9)
1 cup boiling water

2 eggs, beaten
2 tablespoons honey
2 tablespoons fine cornmeal
¹/₄ cup sweet goldenrod blossoms*

Combine all ingredients thoroughly and pour into a well-greased casserole. Sprinkle the top with additional hickory nut meats and bake in a preheated 350° F oven for 1 hour. Serve hot.

*Seeds, raisins, or any other edible blossom may be substituted for goldenrod blossoms.

BLACK WALNUT-MAPLE
COOKIES (yields 3 to 4 dozen large, soft cookies)

1 cup nut butter (see page 9)

2 cups maple sugar

2 large eggs

1 cup shelled dried black walnuts,
  chopped

2 cups cattail flour (see page 66)

2 1/2 cups potato flour (see page 66)

1 teaspoon wood ashes (see page 4)

1 cup hot water

In a large bowl gradually cream together all ingredients. Drop the batter by teaspoonfuls onto greased cookie sheets. Sprinkle the tops with additional nuts if desired. Bake in a preheated 350° F oven for 20 minutes.

BEECHNUT PIE (serves 8)

1 uncooked 9-inch pie shell or 2 cups
  blended cornmeal and nutmeal

3 eggs, whipped until frothy

1 cup beechnut butter (see page 9),
  softened

1 cup light corn syrup

1/2 cup maple sugar

1 cup dried beechnut meats

Prepare a 9-inch pie shell of your favorite pastry recipe, or press blended corn meal and nutmeal evenly into a well-greased pie plate.

Cream together the whipped eggs and beechnut butter, gradually adding the corn syrup and maple sugar. Turn into the prepared pie shell and bake in a preheated 325° F oven for 35 minutes. Remove the pie from the oven and cover the top evenly with the beechnut meats. Return the pie to the oven and bake for another 20 minutes.

This pie recipe can be adapted easily to different nuts. (For Black Walnut Pie, substitute 1 cup dark corn syrup.)

CRANBERRY-WALNUT CAKES (serves 6 to 8)

1 cup cranberries, chopped

3/4 cup shelled dried black walnuts,
  chopped

1 egg, beaten with 1 teaspoon water

1/2 cup honey

2 cups fine cornmeal

1 cup cattail flour (see page 66)

Gradually add each ingredient to the cornmeal and flour, blending thoroughly into a smooth batter. Lighten with additional warm water if the batter seems too heavy or thick. Pour into a well-greased loaf pan (9" x 5") and bake in a preheated 350° F oven for 1 hour. Or spoon into 10 to 12 greased muffin cups and bake until golden on top—about 25 minutes.

BEECHNUT-CURRANT CAKES (yields 12)

1 tablespoon wood ashes (see page 4)
2 cups boiling water
1 cup dried currants
1 cup dried beechnut meats, broken
3 cups fine cornmeal

1 cup beechnut flour (see page 66)
1 cup maple sugar
2 eggs, beaten
3 tablespoons nut butter (see page 9)

Stir the wood ashes into the boiling water and pour this over the currants. Let stand for 15 minutes to cool. Mix together the remaining ingredients; blend in the currants and water. Spread the batter evenly in a greased pan (9" x 9" x 5") and bake for 45 minutes in a preheated 350° F oven. Cool slightly and cut into 12 squares.

MEATLESS PEMMICAN (serves 12)

1/2 cup raisins
1/2 cup peanuts
1/2 cup hickory nuts
1/2 cup dried apples

1/2 cup dried pumpkin or squash
1/2 cup acorn or cornmeal
1/3 cup honey or maple syrup

In order to make sure that the acorn or cornmeal is bone-dry, spread it in a thin layer on a cookie sheet and place it in a warm oven for 15 to 30 minutes, checking frequently. The oven should be at the lowest possible setting. Then combine the dry ingredients and either chop them with a knife or grind them coarsely through a food grinder. Add the honey or maple syrup and blend thoroughly. Divide the mixture into 1/4-cup portions, press into cakes, and store in the refrigerator for use as a high-energy trail snack.

Indians traditionally made these small pressed cakes out of shredded bear, buffalo, or deer meat combined with suet, nuts, and dried fruits or berries.

Berries and Fruits

Native Americans utilized over 250 species of berries and fruits, which they ate raw, used in cooking their foods, mashed for various fruit drinks, and dried for winter additives to their breads, soups, puddings, and pemmicans (dried foods).

The chief nutritive value of berries lies in the minerals and carbohydrates they contain. They are also a rich source of vitamins A and C. To obtain the maximum vitamin benefit, berries should be eaten raw and can be enjoyed fresh in cereals and as complements to other dishes.

Certain wild berries, however, are best cooked to render them less toxic, or sweetened to improve their taste. Cooking also helps to separate certain berries from their large seeds.

AMERICAN CRANBERRY (*Vaccinium macrocarpon*) is a slender, creeping, ovalleaved botanical found growing in northeastern swamps and open bogs. The ripe, shiny berries are tasty raw and have excellent keeping qualities. Traditionally, the cranberry flavored many autumn and winter native foods.

BARBERRY (*Berberis vulgaris, B. canadensis*) bark, leaves, twigs, and fruit are enjoyed by deer, rabbits, and game birds. Fragrant masses of yellow flowers in the spring, amid glossy green leaves through summer, turn to gold and scarlet in late autumn beside the orange-crimson berries, which have one to three shiny brown seeds inside. Both Indians and settlers dried the berries (though they are delicious and tangy raw) for many winter uses and flavor additives. A delightful drink is made by stewing these berries. From them many tarts, preserves, jellies, and pies are derived. The berries are high in pectin and are useful to add to sweeter, blander fruits (such as apples and peaches) to pique their taste. The bitter roots are boiled and used as a healthful, tonic laxative and blood purifier (1 teaspoon powdered root bark in 1 cup water). They are used externally as a lotion to treat various skin diseases. The Indians also made a tea from the leaves and drank it for relief from rheumatism. In addition, they chewed the roots.

BAYBERRY or Candleberry (*Myrica pensylvanica* and 7 native spp.). This is a coastal shrub indigenous to the U.S. The shiny, evergreen aromatic leaves of *Myrica* were used in tanning leather and were dried to keep as a spice (the flavoring is subtle and superb). It has gray bark on radiating branches; the flowers appear in spring clusters before the leaves. Numerous game birds, wild duck, and foxes feed on the berries. Bayberry leaves were a condiment and spice readily available to native Americans. Gather 1 quart fresh leaves, wash them, and spread them to dry, away from the sun or covered. When thoroughly dry and crisp, store in airtight jars. Before using, crumble them into small pieces and blend into cooking sauces, chowders, and stews.

BEARBERRY, Kinnikinnick, Mealberry, Upland Cranberry (*Arctostaphylos uva-ursi*). A widely distributed member of the heath family, bearberry is a trailing, perennial shrub with green, odorless, leathery foliage. Pink, inconspicuous, bell-like blossoms in terminal clusters ripen in autumn to dull red-orange berries. Bearberry is especially sought by the northern black bears in spring. The blandly dry, red berries are good survival food raw, but improve in taste with cooking, especially when mixed with other fruits. The dried and pulverized leaves have been an interest-

BEARBERRY
Arctostaphylos uva-ursi

BEACH PLUM
Prunus maritima

ing frontier tobacco for centuries, both alone and in "herbal tobacco" smoking remedies, as learned from the Indians. The dried leaves are also used for an astringent winter tea with a pleasant bitter taste considered soothing to stomach digestion. (Steep 1 teaspoon dried leaves for 5 minutes.)

BEACH PLUM *(Prunus maritima)* is a native perennial of the rose family. This low, straggling, spring-flowering shrub is indigenous to the North Atlantic coastal regions. It prefers sandy soil and is capable of withstanding the rough maritime climate. Its small, juicy fruits are within easy reach for autumn picking.

BLUE COHOSH, Squaw Root, Papoose Root *(Caulophyllum thalictroides)*. This is a shady woodland tall-stemmed plant with small greenish flowers in April and May and round bluish seeds in August (an excellent coffee substitute when roasted). A boiled decoction of the root was a noted Indian remedy for fever, while many tribes used the warm tea made from the root infusion to aid in childbirth.

BLUE COHOSH
Caulophyllum thalictroides

BUFFALO BERRY
Shepherdia canadensis

BLUEBERRIES (*Vaccinium angustifolium* and various spp.) are a member of the widespread heath family, most of which favor acid soil and light shade. With as many uses to the Amerindians as they have to us today, blueberries were primarily enjoyed raw, preferably "picked before the dew is off." Dried or charred for preservation against winter needs, they were essential to many of the hunting and gathering cultures. They are also the source of a wonderful blue-gray dye; mixed with nutgalls, they produce a rich brown dye or ink.

BUFFALO BERRIES (*Shepherdia canadensis* with 3 var. native only to the U.S.) are a favorite food of black bears, quail, and song birds. Indians dried these like currants, to be used with buffalo meat. They have small yellow flowers with green oval leaves that are silvery underneath. Small, round orange-scarlet berries are translucent and contain saponin. The berries are sweetened by frost.

CHOKECHERRY
Prunus virginiana

CHOKECHERRY (*Prunus virginiana*), WILD BLACK CHERRY (*P. serotina*). One of the most widely distributed trees on the North American continent. Long clusters of flowers blossom in late spring and usually produce abundant red to black fruits, tart and tasty, about the size of large peas; excellent raw. Avoid eating the leaves and the kernels, as they are toxic.

FALSE SOLOMON'S SEAL, False Spikenard, Scurvyberries (*Smilacina racemosa*), is a showy woodland plant of the lily family, noted for its terminal blossom clusters, which bloom in the spring and ripen in autumn to small clusters of aromatic red berries. These are delightful eaten raw or used as seasonings; they are somewhat cathartic and should be eaten in moderation.

GROUND-CHERRY, Chinese Lantern, Strawberry Tomato, Husk-Tomato (*Physalis pubescens*), is a widespread annual weed of the nightshade family. These ornamental vines produce the bright-orange papery husk (resembling an Oriental lantern) that droops by autumn. Each husk contains one bright-orange, smooth, many-seeded berry, which is much like a tiny tomato, about $\frac{1}{2}$ inch in diameter. The berry's milky, pleasant flavor when fully ripe makes it a delight to eat fresh. But unless the berries are fully ripe, they have an unpleasant taste. This worthwhile fruit complements any dish or relish and was dried by many tribes for winter seasonings. Suitable for preserves, jams, jellies, pies, and sauces, ground-cherries do require pectin or the addition of a tart, more acid companion fruit.

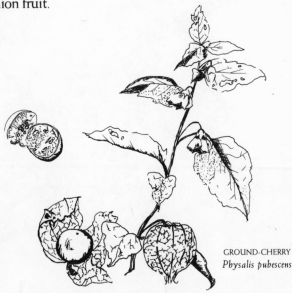

GROUND-CHERRY
Physalis pubescens

HIGHBUSH CRANBERRY or Squawbush (*Viburnum trilobum* — *not* related to the cranberry) is a tall shrub 6 to 10 feet high. The leaves are opposite, toothed, and terminate in three lobes, slightly resembling the maple. The white flowers are in clusters. Bright-red berries sweeten after frost, are high in vitamin C, and cling during the winter. The bark is a New and Old World medicinal antispasmodic used to treat asthma, epilepsy, and convulsions. It is gathered in the spring.

JUNEBERRY, Shadbush, Serviceberry (*Amelanchier canadensis* and var. spp.). These deciduous shrubs are native to temperate North America. Our earliest blooming spring shrubs, their juicy blackish berries are usually ripe in June. They must be harvested early, as they are highly prized by birds and woodland creatures.

JUNIPER BERRIES (*Juniperus communis* and spp.). These gray-blue aromatic berries were prized in Northwest Coast cultures as a secret ingredient of so many of their varied and succulent recipes. The distinctive flavors of salmon, deer, elk, and bear were enhanced by this woodsy fragrance. Also a popular winter flavoring used by Eastern Woodlands tribes, juniper berries were widely used in tea and to flavor natural medicines and smoking mixtures.

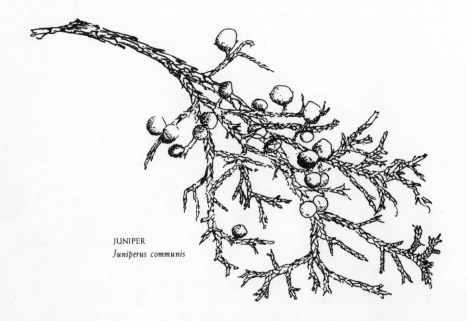

JUNIPER
Juniperus communis

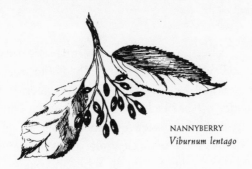

NANNYBERRY
Viburnum lentago

NANNYBERRY, Sheepberry, Wild Raisin *(Viburnum lentago)*, is a spring-flowering viburnum shrub. The white blossom clusters give way to flat clusters of oval, green summer berries ripening to blue blackberries on coral-red stems. The drooping fruits are juicy, contain a solitary stone, and are sweetened by early frosts.

NIGHTSHADE *(Solanaceae* spp.). Bittersweet berries of the Solanaceae (nightshade) family are toxic fresh, especially when underripe. These fruits contain a poisonous alkaloid, solanine, which decreases to a non-toxic state in the ripe fruit and is completely destroyed by heat in cooking. Northeastern tribes cooked the ripe hulled berries in their meat stews. They make a tasty seasoning.

PARTRIDGEBERRY or Squaw Vine *(Mitchella repens)*. This is a creeping evergreen with fragrant white flowers, April to June, in pairs. The scarlet berries are very bland and long-lasting and contain tannin (a substance which preserves tissue). Steeped as a tea, they were used as a tonic as well as an astringent. They have diuretic properties. A tea made of the leaves was used by many tribes (Cherokees, Penobscots) to speed and ease labor in childbirth.

SPICEBUSH, Wild Allspice, Feverbush *(Lindera benzoin)*. This deciduous native shrub of our eastern woodlands prefers damp ground. Its honey-yellow spring blossoms give way to small, spicy yellow-to-red fruits which are something of a delicacy, as not many shrubs set fruit. The berries have excellent keeping qualities if dried; grind coarsely and use in place of conventional pepper.

WILD PLUM *(Prunus americana)* is another native perennial, widespread across temperate North America. Growing as a coarse shrub or small tree, it favors woodland borders, thickets, and the banks of streams. Its spring flowers give way to small red-to-yellow fruits, which are enjoyed throughout late summer, growing sweeter in autumn.

WINTERGREEN, Checkerberry, Teaberry (*Gaultheria procumbens*), is a tiny creeping shrub of infertile woodlands, growing especially under evergreens. The leaves were the original source of oil of wintergreen but have been displaced by the wider use of black birch twigs, which contain greater quantities of this oil. Both the leaves and the berries are refreshing eaten raw. They contain a compound similar to aspirin and can be effective in reducing fever and relieving minor aches and pains.

WINTERGREEN
Gaultheria procumbens

BEACH PLUM JAM (*yields eight 6-ounce jars*)

1 quart select beach plums	8 cups sugar
1 cup water	sterile glass jars

Cook the beach plums in the water in a covered saucepan over low heat for 15 minutes, or until soft. Remove from heat; cool slightly. Seed the plums, but do not mash. Return the fruit to the juice in the saucepan. Add the sugar while boiling; stir constantly for 15 minutes.

Skim the froth from the jam. Ladle the jam into glass jars, and seal immediately with ¼ inch liquid paraffin.

STEWED WILD CHERRIES (serves 8)

1 quart wild black cherries, stoned,   1 cup maple syrup
   cracked, and cherry kernel saved   1 cup cider

Simmer the wild cherries with their kernels plus the syrup and cider in a large covered crock, stirring occasionally, for 30 minutes. Serve either hot or cooled over puddings, or to flavor cornmeal dishes.

WILD GRAPE BUTTER
(OR WILD PLUM OR APPLE BUTTER)

Pick the wild grapes before the first light frost. Stem and wash them, then cover them with water in a large covered pot and bring to a boil. Simmer for 30 minutes or until their skins pop. Stir and mash the grapes as they cook. Pour off the grape juice to sweeten with honey, and drink.

Sieve the remaining grape pulp to remove the seeds, and puree. Add an equal measure of maple sugar or honey, blending all in a bean-pot. Bake in a preheated 325° F oven, stirring occasionally, for 3 hours. Seal in hot, sterilized jars.

Applesauce and grape puree may be combined to create yet another tasty butter variation. Wild plum puree and apple butter are also a good combination.

DRIED APPLES, PUMPKIN,
PLUMS, ETC.

Peel and core the harvested fruit. Slice thinly ½ to ¼ inch thick and spread to air-dry on white cloth or muslin, away from the sun, over screens or boards. Turn twice daily. Keep the fruits from touching. Depending on the atmospheric conditions, it can take 6 to 10 days before the fruit is fully dehydrated. The process can be effectively hastened by drying near a fire or in a very low oven. Store in airtight containers.

Dehydration of seasonal fruits and vegetables was, and still is, the most efficient way of putting most of these foods by — safely. Furthermore, these foodstuffs occupy much less space when reduced by natural water loss and are the least changed chemically. They make very nutritious sweet snacks.

INDIAN PUDDING (serves 12)

2 cups raisins or nannyberries
2 cups fine cornmeal
4 cups water
¹/₂ cup nut butter (see page 9)

¹/₂ cup honey
¹/₄ cup Juneberries, fresh or dried
¹/₄ teaspoon ground ginger
¹/₂ teaspoon nutmeg

Toss the raisins (or nannyberries) and cornmeal together gently. Bring the water to a boil with the nut butter in a large saucepan. Gradually add the cornmeal-raisin mixture and simmer, stirring until it thickens — about 15 minutes. Add the remaining ingredients, blending thoroughly. Pour into a 2¹/₂ quart greased casserole. Set the casserole in a pan of water, 1″ or 2″ deep, and bake in a preheated 325° F oven for 2¹/₂ hours. Cool thoroughly before serving. Serve with nut milk (see page 7) or additional nutmeg for topping.

JUNEBERRY
Amelanchier canadensis

BAKED STUFFED APPLES (serves 6)

6 whole, firm apples, cored almost
    through to the bottom
¹/₂ cup dried currants or raisins or fresh
    blueberries

6 spicebush berries, dried and crushed
¹/₂ cup honey

Arrange the apples (in their skins) in a greased baking dish. Blend together the berries and honey and heat. Stuff each apple center pocket with the hot mixture, drizzling some over the skins. Bake in a 300° F oven for 30 minutes, basting once. Serve hot.

Sauces

CRANBERRY SAUCE (yields about 1 quart)

2 pounds cranberries   1 cup maple sugar
1 cup dried black walnut meats, chopped   1 cup cider

Combine all ingredients in a large kettle. Bring to a boil. Cover, reduce the heat, and simmer for 30 minutes, or until the cranberries' skins pop and the mixture looks glassy. Cool slightly, chill, and serve.

CRANBERRY AND WALNUT SAUCE (yields about 3 cups)

1 pound wild cranberries   1 cup maple syrup
2 cups water   2 tablespoons cornstarch, with enough
1/2 pound dried black walnut meats,   water to make it a thick paste
    chopped

Place the cranberries and water in a covered pot, bring to a boil, and simmer until the berries pop. Add the chopped walnuts and syrup, simmer for another 10 minutes, then thicken with cornstarch paste, stirring to blend thoroughly.
   Serve either hot or chilled with turkey, game, or other fowl.

CREAMED BEECHNUT SAUCE (yields about 2 cups)

2 cups water, with 1 tablespoon wood   4 tablespoons fine cornmeal
    ashes (see page 4)   1/2 cup dried beechnut meats
4 tablespoons beechnut butter (see
    page 9)

Bring the water and ashes to a boil, then simmer. Add the nut butter and blend until smooth. Gradually stir in the cornmeal, blending until smooth and thick. Add the nutmeats, and simmer for 2 minutes more. Serve hot to dress and complement roasts, fried fish, or your favorite vegetables.

Tree Essences

MAPLES (*Aceraceae*) are the most distinctive trees and shrubs in North America. There are 12 native species, and over 150 species of maples known. These handsome deciduous trees produce paired, winged fruits and usually have simple opposite leaves; their seeds ripen in spring and early summer. Maple trees are tapped in late winter/early spring, when the days begin to warm but the nights remain frosty cold. The sugaring season can last 3 to 6 weeks (until the trees bud and blossom) with the sap flowing sweet and water-clear. At blossomtime the sap turns to pale amber, and the taste definitely changes. Though sugaring may continue, the product is less desirable, and continued sapping-off would impair the health of the tree. Many myths and legends about the sacred maples have come to us from the Indians. The Mohicans believed that the melting snow caused the spring sap to run in the maples; they considered the snow to be the dripping oil of the Great Celestial Bear, who had been slain by the winter hunters.

Maple Syrup was the Eastern Woodlands Indians' principal confection. Most early accounts of explorations into these cultures mention the use of maple syrup as well as the tapping of various trees near winter's end. Maple syrup and its sugars were greatly favored, and were used to flavor cooked vegetables and fruits and to mellow the flavors of various native stews.

Natural Sugars can be derived from the sap of several other native trees, much the same as the Indians refined them from the maples. In the early spring the three major species of birches were tapped: BLACK BIRCH, Cherry Birch or Sweet Birch (*Betula lenta*), YELLOW BIRCH (*B. lutea*), and WHITE BIRCH (*B. papyrifera*). A number of beverages, liquors, vinegars, syrups, and sugars are easily rendered from these trees.

MAPLES

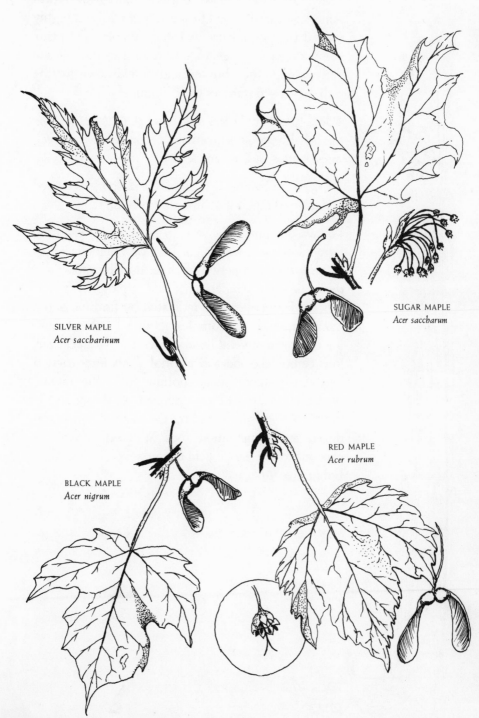

SILVER MAPLE
Acer saccharinum

SUGAR MAPLE
Acer saccharum

BLACK MAPLE
Acer nigrum

RED MAPLE
Acer rubrum

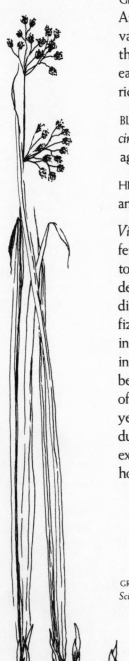

GREAT BULRUSH (*Scirpus validus*), native to North American marshes and freshwater ponds, was highly valued by the Indians. A totally usable food plant, the younger, smaller roots were dug in the fall and early spring, then bruised and boiled down for the rich sugars and starches they contain.

BLACK WALNUT (*Juglans nigra*) and BUTTERNUT (*Juglans cinerea*) also produce quantities of spring sap for beverages, syrups, sugars, and so on.

HICKORY, or Swamp Bitternut (*Carya* spp.), is tapped and utilized much the same way as birch sap.

Vinegars are relatively easy to produce by exposing fermenting saps, syrups, or fruit or vegetable juices to air for a short period of time, usually a few days, depending on temperatures and atmospheric conditions. Fermentation is indicated by frothing and a fizzing noise. It is a complex action whereby the living organism of yeast breaks down the natural sugars into carbon dioxide and alcohol. This interreaction between yeast and sugar continues until the volume of alcohol reaches 12 to 14 percent. At this point the yeast's action is inhibited by the alcohol it has produced, and fermentation stops. When the mixture is exposed to air, acetic acid bacteria oxidize the alcohol to give vinegar.

GREAT BULRUSH
Scirpus validus

CATBRIER
Smilax rotundifolia

Additional Wild Flavorings

BLACK MUSTARD (*Brassica nigra*) is a widespread native perennial used by the Indians as a potherb and seasoning. Its seeds are gathered as they ripen in summer and are dried and ground to be used in place of conventional pepper. It is the principal source of table mustard.

CATBRIER (*Smilax* spp.) is a widely distributed perennial climbing vine. Its pounded roots yield a fine gelatin with a mild taste similar to that of wild sarsaparilla.

COLTSFOOT (*Tussilago farfara*) is a spring-blooming perennial of swamps and stream banks found all across northern North America and sought for its versatile leaves, which may be used as a salt substitute. Roll the large, broad coltsfoot leaf into a tight ball and dry thoroughly before a fire; then burn. The resulting ashes are very salty and can be used to season many dishes to taste. Highly prized by numerous Indian tribes, coltsfoot was especially in demand among various vegetarian peoples, to such a degree that it became the object of intertribal warfare among West Coast tribes.

CORIANDER (*Coriandrum sativum*) is a pungent herb of the parsley family, cultivated for centuries for its flavorful seeds. It is still cultivated by the Zunis, who use the fragrant foliage in salads, and the seeds to season meats and chilies.

GARLIC MUSTARD (*Alliaria officinalis*) is a persistent biennial herb of our countrysides and open woods, where it has naturalized (after introduction from Eurasia). This tall, white blossoming botanical may be used to lend a garlic flavor to many dishes; it is a fine vegetable raw or slightly steamed. Use its leaves, blossoms, and young seed pods throughout the spring and summer.

GARLIC MUSTARD SAUCE (serves 4 to 6)

2 cups fresh garlic mustard leaves,
  chopped coarsely
½ cup nut oil (see page 7) or corn oil

1 teaspoon ground dried spicebush
  berries

Blend all ingredients together thoroughly. Cook in a heavy iron skillet over moderate heat for 5 minutes or until the garlic mustard is limp and warmed through. Serve over fish.

MILKWEED (Asclepias syriaca) blossoms and buds make fragrant flavorings and thickeners for meats, soups, and stews. For use as a seasoning they should be dried.

MINT LEAVES (Mentha spp.) complement almost all wild foods and game, but are especially good for seasoning meats.

ONION, GARLIC, and LEEK (Allium spp.), all of which may be found growing wild, are flavorful and nutritious raw or cooked with native food preparations.

PURPLE AVENS or Water Avens (Geum rivale) is a low, blossoming perennial of swamps, meadows, and bogs, widely spread across North America and sought for its chocolate-flavored roots. The roots are acid and slightly astringent, but when well sugared, they are a tasty seasoning.

SASSAFRAS (Sassafras albidum), the fragrant deciduous shrub/tree, native to northeastern North America, was much prized and well used by the native Americans. The aromatic bark, roots, and leaves were used in teas and medicinal drinks. The Choctaws taught the early settlers to grind dried sassafras leaves into a powder that would sweeten and thicken their stews. This subsequently became the flavorful essence of Creole cooking, the filé that forms the base of gumbo.

FILÉ POWDER

Gather young sassafras leaves and spread them to dry in a layer on a screen. When leaves are crisp and crumbly, grind them until powdery, sieve and store in glass jars. Use 1 tablespoon filé powder per pot of stew or gumbo. Remove pot from heat and slowly add the powder, stirring well. *Do not add filé while the gumbo is cooking*, or it will become stringy and unappealing.

SHEEP SORREL *(Rumex acetosella)* is a widespread weed favoring sour soil. Its leaves are useful as a seasoning and thickener; boiled, they make a flavorful beverage similar to lemonade. Sorrel especially complements fish and potatoes.

SHEPHERD'S PURSE *(Capsella bursa-pastoris)* is a vigorous wild plant spread all across our country and used by many tribes as a flavorful potherb and peppery seasoning. California Indians used the seeds as a source of ground meal. The seeds are gathered as the small pods ripen in autumn, and are used in soups and stews.

SWEET COLTSFOOT *(Petasites palmata)* was sought as a potherb, tobacco, medicine, and tea. Like coltsfoot *(Tussilago farfara)*, its ashes may be used as a salt substitute.

WILD GINGER
Asarum canadense

WILD GINGER *(Asarum canadense)* is a low-growing woodland plant found throughout the northern United States. Its long, slender roots are a sought-after flavoring, confection, and medicine. They are easily dug and are used fresh or dried for their unique flavoring qualities. In some states wild ginger is on the protected species list; if harvesting is permitted, do so sparingly.

WILD SARSAPARILLA *(Aralia nudicaulis* and spp.) is a native perennial plant widely used by many tribes for a variety of preparations, but principally for its flavorful rootstock.

II

NATIVE SOUPS

Soups complement and extend a meal; they are a delicious means of stretching limited quantities of foodstuffs. The best soups are the homemade stocks derived from fresh or dried produce and herbs. The native Americans evolved numerous concoctions of the wonderful foods inhabiting their regional environments.

JERUSALEM ARTICHOKE (*Helianthus tuberosus*) is a native sunflower that develops edible tubers. It grows 3 to 10 feet tall, is slender, branching, and persistent, and thrives in dense clumps in the wild (as well as in cultivated areas). It has slender, pointed leaves and produces many flowerheads, 2 to 3 inches in diameter, with small quantities of edible seeds. This plant has been a popular vegetable among the Indians for many centuries. Because of its hardiness and tastiness it was also cultivated extensively by the colonists and was enjoyed as a delicacy.

Jerusalem artichoke tubers are harvested in late fall; shaped like knobby sweet potatoes, they grow from 3 to 5 inches long. Their sweet juiciness is reminiscent of water chestnuts and potatoes. A truly versatile vegetable, the tubers can be used like either of these or like carrots. More nutritious than potatoes and lower in starch, these tubers are so digestible that they are considered excellent food for babies and invalids (and everyone in between). They are delicious raw, eaten in salads, briefly cooked and pickled, or boiled, roasted, creamed, or fried, like potatoes. They make excellent food for diabetics.

JERUSALEM ARTICHOKE SOUP (serves 8)

1 pound Jerusalem artichokes, scrubbed
6 cups water
3 scallions, sliced (including tops)

2 tablespoons dillseed
1 tablespoon chopped fresh dillweed
3 eggs, beaten lightly

Boil the Jerusalem artichokes in the water in a covered saucepan for 25 minutes, or until tender. Drain, reserving the liquid, and slice the artichokes in half. Scoop the meat out of the skins and mash until it makes a smooth puree. Combine the puree, scallions, water, and seasonings, and simmer for 15 minutes.

Pour several spoonfuls of hot soup into the beaten eggs, stirring well. Slowly add the egg mixture to the hot soup, stirring over low heat for 1 more minute; serve.

EVENING PRIMROSE (*Oenothera biennis*) is a favorite biennial flowering plant with edible leaves and roots. Gather first-year roots before the plant blossoms.

EVENING PRIMROSE ROOT SOUP (serves 6)

2 cups quartered evening primrose roots
2 cups diced Jerusalem artichokes
2 quarts water
3 wild onions, halved

6 bayberry leaves, dried and crumbled
1/2 teaspoon grated dried spicebush berries
3 wild leeks, diced
2 tablespoons chopped fresh dillweed

Combine all ingredients (except the dill) in a large soup kettle. Cover and simmer for 40 minutes, add the dill, and simmer for 10 minutes more. Season to taste and serve hot.

SQUASH (*Cucurbita* spp.) was almost as important as corn to the Iroquois and other Eastern Woodlands tribes. It was versatile and nourishing and was also ceremonially important. The rattles created and used by the medicine societies were fashioned of the summer crookneck squash and the long-necked calabashes (gourds). Squash was generally baked whole, especially the rich, sweet-meated hard-shelled varieties: buttercup, acorn, and butternut. Favored seasonings were honey, maple syrup, and animal fats. The yellow summer varieties of squash were mostly boiled (often with their blossoms, to thicken the broth) and blended into smooth, fragrant soups.

YELLOW SQUASH SOUP (serves 8)

2 pounds or 2 medium yellow squash,
    cubed
2 scallions or wild onions, sliced
    (including tops)
1 tablespoon honey
1 tablespoon sunflower seed oil (see
    page 8)

1 quart water
1 tablespoon chopped fresh dillweed
garnish: shelled sunflower seeds or toasted
    squash seeds

Simmer the squash, scallions, honey, and oil in the water in a large covered pot for 30 minutes, or until the squash is tender. Cool slightly,
mash to a smooth puree, and add the dill. Return to heat and simmer
for another 5 minutes. Add more water to thin if desired. Serve either
hot or cold with garnishes.

CLOVER SOUP (serves 6)

2 cups clover blossoms and leaves, fresh
    or dried
2 small wild onions, chopped
4 tablespoons sunflower seed butter (see
    page 8)
1 quart water
12 groundnuts, or 3 medium potatoes,
    quartered
chopped fresh dillweed to taste
spicebush berries, dried, grated over soup
    to taste

Sauté the clover blossoms and leaves and
the chopped onions in the sunflower seed
butter. Add the water, and groundnuts,
and seasonings. Simmer, covered, for 20
minutes. Serve hot.

WILD ONION
Allium cernuum

SCALLION SOUP (serves 6)

8 scallions, sliced (including tops)
8 dried juniper berries
6 cups water
1 tablespoon chopped fresh coriander

Combine all ingredients in a large pot and simmer, covered, for 40 minutes. Serve hot.

SUNFLOWER SEED SOUP (serves 6)

2 cups shelled sunflower seeds
3 scallions, chopped (including tops)
6 cups water
1 teaspoon chopped fresh dillweed

Simmer all ingredients in a large covered pot, stirring occasionally, for 30 minutes. Serve hot.

FRESH TOMATO (OR POTATO) SOUP (serves 10)

4 pounds ripe tomatoes or potatoes, diced
1 cooking apple, peeled, cored, and quartered
2 yellow onions, chopped
1/2 cup fresh mint leaves, chopped
2 quarts water
1 tablespoon sunflower seed oil (see page 8)
1 tablespoon fine cornmeal
1/2 teaspoon chopped fresh basil
2 bayberry leaves
1 cup chopped fresh dillweed

Place all ingredients except the last three in a large kettle. Cover and simmer slowly, stirring occasionally, for 2 hours. Add the basil, bayberry leaves, and dill, and simmer for 10 minutes more. Serve hot.

CORN CHOWDER (serves 8)

3 cups dried corn kernels
6 cups water or meat stock
1 potato, diced
1 onion, chopped
1 green pepper, chopped
2 tablespoons nut butter (see page 9)
1/2 pound fresh mushrooms, sliced
1 tablespoon chopped fresh dillweed
garnish: chopped dillweed or seasonal herbs of your choice

Soak the corn in the water (or stock) overnight in a large, covered kettle. Bring to a boil, then simmer, covered, for 15 minutes. Add the remaining ingredients (except the mushrooms and dill) and simmer for another 30 minutes. Add the sliced muchrooms. Steam with the lid on for another 5 minutes. Garnish, and serve hot.

CORN SOUP (serves 8)

kernels from 2 ears dried flint corn
8 cups water
2 scallions, chopped (including tops)
10 juniper berries, dried

one 2-inch strip fatback, thinly sliced
½ pound dried bear meat or venison or
  beef, etc.

Soak the corn in 2 cups of the water overnight in a large, covered kettle. Add the remaining ingredients, bring to a boil, and simmer, covered, for 3 to 4 hours until the corn is tender. Serve hot.

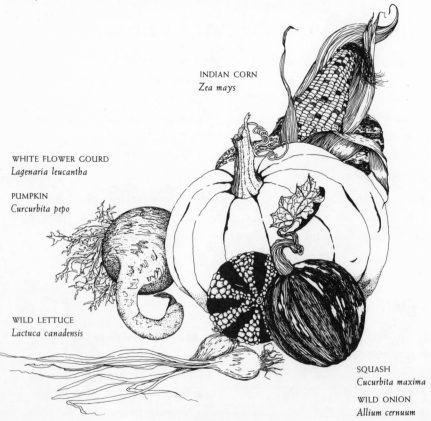

INDIAN CORN
Zea mays

WHITE FLOWER GOURD
Lagenaria leucantha

PUMPKIN
Curcurbita pepo

WILD LETTUCE
Lactuca canadensis

SQUASH
Cucurbita maxima

WILD ONION
Allium cernuum

BLACK WALNUT AND PUMPKIN SOUP (serves 4 to 6)

1 small pumpkin (about 12 inches in
    diameter)
1 cup black walnuts, chopped
maple syrup (to taste)

1 quart water
garnish: roasted pumpkin seeds and
    chopped walnuts

Roast the whole washed pumpkin in a preheated 325° F oven for 1 hour
(or until the skin wrinkles and is easily pierced with a sharp stick); remove the pumpkin and cool slightly. Cut the pumpkin open and spoon
out the seeds (save and spread in a pan to toast). Spoon out the pumpkin
meat into a saucepan and mash it with the walnuts and syrup, adding
enough water to liquefy to the desired soup consistency. Mix well and
simmer, covered, for 3 to 5 minutes. Serve garnished with roasted
pumpkin seeds and a spoonful of chopped walnuts.

    This excellent taste combination is very high in vitamins and min-
erals and is a rich source of carbohydrates and proteins.

HAZELNUT SOUP (serves 6)

2 cups ground dried hazelnuts
5 cups water
1 tablespoon honey

2 scallions, diced (including tops)
2 tablespoons chopped fresh parsley

Simmer all ingredients together in a covered saucepan, stirring frequently, for 1 hour. Serve hot in small servings, as this is a rich soup.

TROUT STEW (serves 10)

two 3-pound trout, cleaned
2 large potatoes, quartered
2 large onions, quartered
2 quarts water
10 juniper berries

1 pound spinach or purslane, chopped
11 fresh mint leaves
2 tablespoons nut butter (see page 9)
garnish: chopped fresh parsley and
    dillweed

Combine the first five ingredients in a large covered kettle and simmer for 30 minutes. Carefully remove the fish, peel, bone, and return the trout meat to the kettle. Continue to simmer for 20 minutes more. Mash the juniper berries with a spoon against the side of the kettle. Add the greens and nut butter and simmer for 10 minutes more. Serve steaming hot with chopped fresh parsley and dillweed.

EASTERN BOX TURTLE

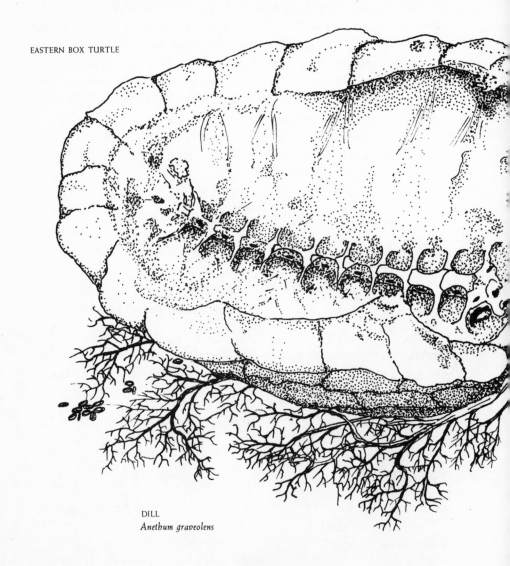

DILL
Anethum graveolens

TURTLES and turtle eggs were prized by many tribes. Favored species were the snappers, wood turtles, and painted turtles, and the giant sea turtles far south. Turtle broth was considered a remedy for sore throats and was a special food for young babies. The turtle shells became musical instruments (rattles), ceremonial symbols, and serving bowls long before there were pottery or wooden eating vessels. Easy hunting, the turtle has long been associated with all Indian cultures.

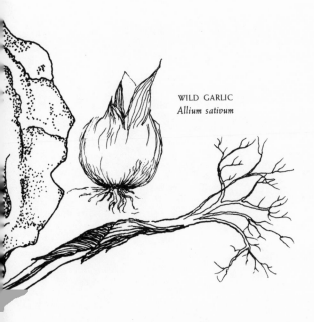

WILD GARLIC
Allium sativum

TURTLE SOUP (serves 4)

1 pound turtle or terrapin meat
2 scallions, sliced (including tops)

3 quarts water
1 tablespoon chopped fresh dillweed

Combine all ingredients in a large pot and simmer for 2 hours. Remove the meat, cool slightly, dice; return the meat to the broth. Add more water as necessary. Simmer for 1 more hour, or until tender. Serve hot.

III

❧

NATIVE
VEGETABLES

The early Americans' relationship to their foods and methods of harvesting was also intricately interwoven with their human and spiritual relationships. The Indians' kinship to the plant world was a product of centuries of accumulated knowledge. Much can be understood about a culture through analyzing its seasonal diet.

These select recipes "skim the surface" in order to focus on the Amerindians' respect for their environment and their resourcefulness. Most of these botanicals are widely available and possess great food value.

JERUSALEM ARTICHOKE SALAD (serves 6)

1 pound Jerusalem artichokes, scrubbed and diced	1/2 cup cider vinegar
	1 tablespoon honey
2 scallions, diced finely (including tops)	1 tablespoon chopped fresh mint leaves
1/2 cup nut oil (see page 7)	2 cups salad greens

Place the Jerusalem artichokes and scallions in a large salad bowl. Add the nut oil, vinegar, honey, and mint leaves. Toss thoroughly. Marinate at room temperature for 1 hour. Add the salad greens, toss again, and serve.

JERUSALEM ARTICHOKE
Helianthus tuberosus

(enlarged.)

SPICED JERUSALEM ARTICHOKES (serves 8)

1 pound Jerusalem artichokes,
    scrubbed and sliced
½ cup nut oil (see page 7)
2 cloves wild garlic, chopped

2 tablespoons chopped chives
2 tablespoons chopped fresh dillweed
¼ cup cider vinegar

Boil the Jerusalem artichokes in water to cover for 20 minutes. Drain.
Combine the Jerusalem artichokes and the nut oil, garlic, chives, and
dill in a skillet; sauté, stirring, for 15 minutes. Add the vinegar and
simmer for 5 minutes longer. Serve hot.

ROAST JERUSALEM ARTICHOKES (serves 8)

1 pound Jerusalem artichokes
nut oil (see page 7)

Wipe the Jerusalem artichokes with nut oil and wrap them individually
in foil, or place them directly, unwrapped, in the glowing coals of a
wood fire. Roast for 10 minutes, turn, and roast for 10 minutes more.
Serve hot, split in half, with nut butter (page 9) or nut oil (page 7) to
accent the taste.

LAMB'S QUARTERS (Chenopodium album) is a
nutritious member of the goosefoot family,
a relative of spinach. It is one of the earliest
spring greens to harvest. This wild relative
is tasty all summer long and into autumn,
when the leaves are still delicious. Brought
centuries ago from Europe, this hardy annual
has spread throughout our country.

A multitude of tiny black seeds (up to
75,000 per single plant) are easily harvested
in late summer. These nutritious "poppy
seeds" from lamb's quarters can be used as
seasoning, garnishes, and cereal or flour
additives.

This bountiful cosmopolitan plant seems
to be cultivated in some areas, it grows so
profusely.

LAMB'S QUARTERS
Chenopodium album

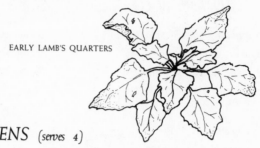

EARLY LAMB'S QUARTERS

LAMB'S QUARTERS (GOOSEFOOT) GREENS (serves 4)

4 cups lamb's quarter leaves
1 tablespoon nut butter (see page 9)

½ cup water
diced scallions (to taste)

Combine all ingredients in a covered saucepan and simmer for 5 minutes, or until the greens are tender. Serve hot.

NASTURTIUM (*Nasturtium officinale* and spp.), a member of the watercress family, is a tasty and colorful addition to any summertime cold plate. As a garnish, the nasturtium is hearty and highly nutritious. The blossoms, buds, leaves, and seeds taste like radishes. "When the covered wagons moved west across the Plains, the settlers found a kind of nasturtium growing wild. They named it Indian Cress because tribes of the area used both the blossoms and leaves to give their green salads a special pungency."*

NASTURTIUM SALAD (serves 4)

1 cup young nasturtium leaves
1 cup nasturtium buds and blossoms

2 cups mixed greens
1 scallion, chopped (including tops)

Dressing

⅓ cup sunflower seed oil (see page 8)
¼ cup cider vinegar

1 tablespoon honey
1 teaspoon chopped fresh dillweed

Combine the dressing ingredients in a glass jar and shake to blend. Let stand at room temperature for a while to develop flavor.

Combine all the salad ingredients in a large bowl and toss. Dress, toss again, and serve.

*Yeffe Kimball and Jean Anderson, *The Art of American Indian Cooking* (Garden City, N.Y.: Doubleday & Co., Inc., 1965), p. 117.

SALAD OF WILD GREENS (serves 6)

2 scallions, sliced (including tops)
1 quart watercress sprigs
1 quart wild lettuce leaves

1 cup wood sorrel leaves and blossoms*
1 cup fresh mint leaves
$^1\!/_2$ cup chopped fresh dillweed

Dressing:

$^1\!/_2$ cup vinegar
$^1\!/_2$ cup nut oil (see page 7)

Toss all the salad ingredients together in a large wooden bowl and dress.

PURSLANE
Portulaca oleracea

PURSLANE SALAD (serves 8)

2 quarts purslane, washed twice
1 cup boiling water
1 medium onion, sliced thinly
2 ripe tomatoes, cubed

$^1\!/_4$ cup chopped fresh dillweed
$^1\!/_2$ cup cidar vinegar
$^1\!/_3$ cup nut oil (see page 7)

Steam the purslane in the boiling water in a covered saucepan for 5 minutes. Drain and cool. Add the remaining ingredients to the purslane in a large wooden bowl. Toss thoroughly. Serve.

*Wood sorrel should be eaten in moderation because of its high oxalic acid content.

YOUNG MILKWEED SPEARS (serves 6)

2 quarts young milkweed spears (picked
   before 10 inches tall and before
   leaves unfurl; plant becomes toxic
   as it matures)

1 tablespoon wood ashes (see page 4)
3 cups water
garnish: nut butter (see page 9) or nut
   milk (see page 7)

Steam these young plant tops (do not boil) with the wood ashes in 1 cup water in a covered saucepan for 4 to 5 minutes. Pour off this first bath, rinse thoroughly, and steam again in 1 cup clear, fresh water without wood ashes for 4 to 5 minutes. Rinse and steam again in 1 cup water for 4 to 5 minutes. Serve either hot or chilled (like asparagus) with complements of nut butter or nut milk topping.

MILKWEED BUDS AND BLOSSOMS (serves 4)

1 quart freshly gathered milkweed buds
   and blossom clumps
1 clove wild garlic, chopped

1/2 cup water
1 tablespoon maple syrup (optional)

Steam the milkweed buds and blossoms with the garlic in a covered saucepan for 15 minutes. Stir thoroughly and add maple syrup if desired. Serve either hot or cold; this spicy, fragrant vegetable is delicious either way. Also excellent served as a seasoning and flavor enhancer to other vegetable and fish dishes.

STEAMED YOUNG MILKWEED PODS (serves 8)

3 quarts young (tiny) whole milkweed
   pods, up to 1 1/2 inch long only*
2 cups boiling water

1 scallion, diced (including top)
2 tablespoons maple syrup

Combine all ingredients in a covered saucepan and simmer (do not boil) for 25 minutes, stirring occasionally. Serve either hot or cold. These crisp, spicy pods make good garnishes and finger foods as well as a very tasty vegetable. The taste is reminiscent of okra.

*Milkweed pods this size can be harvested for almost 6 weeks through July and early August.

MILKWEED PODS VINAIGRETTE (serves 10 to 12)

1 quart young whole milkweed pods
  (under ¹/₂ inch long)
1 cup milkweed buds and blossoms
  (optional)

2 cups small white onions, peeled
1 quart water
¹/₂ cup maple syrup

Combine all ingredients in an enamel pot and bring to a boil. Simmer, covered, for 25 minutes. Stir occasionally. Drain and rinse with cold water. Place ingredients in a crock and prepare marinade.

Marinade:

2 cups chopped pimentos
1 cup chopped fresh dillweed

1 quart cider vinegar
¹/₂ quart corn oil

Blend all ingredients together thoroughly and pour over mixture in the crock. Stir gently. Cover and refrigerate overnight to enhance flavors before serving. This tasty, colorful dish is a favorite in July and August, one worth putting by in extra amounts for winter enjoyment!

BUTTERED NETTLES (serves 6)

1 scallion, diced (including top)
2 tablespoons sunflower seed oil (see
  page 8)

2 quarts young nettle tops*
¹/₂ cup boiling water
¹/₃ cup sunflower seed butter (see page 8)

In a medium saucepan, sauté the scallion in the sunflower seed oil over medium heat for 3 minutes. Add the nettles, boiling water, and seed butter. Stir thoroughly, and simmer, covered, for 20 minutes. Serve steaming hot with the broth. A highly nutritious vegetable and soup stock.

BUTTERED BEECH LEAVES (serves 4)

2 cups young beech leaves† (newly
  collected, as they wilt rapidly)
³/₄ cup boiling water

1 clove wild garlic, crushed
1 tablespoon nut butter (see page 9)

*Cooking destroys the nettles' stinging properties.
†Beech leaves should be picked by the leaf stalk (petiole); eat the leaf blade and discard the stalk.

Combine all ingredients in a medium saucepan, stir thoroughly to blend, cover, and simmer for 8 minutes. Serve hot as an appetizer or side vegetable. Eat with the fingers.

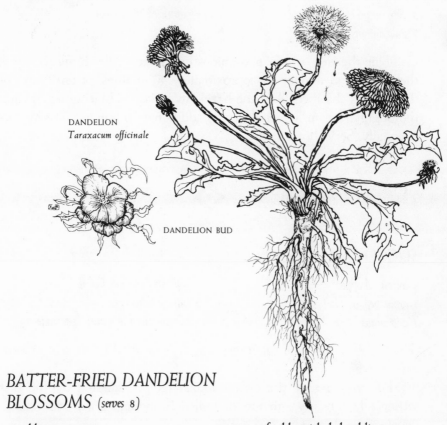

DANDELION
Taraxacum officinale

DANDELION BUD

BATTER-FRIED DANDELION BLOSSOMS (serves 8)

1 tablespoon water
2 eggs
¹/₄ cup nut oil (see page 7)

2 quarts freshly picked dandelion
blossoms, washed and dried*
1 ¹/₂ cups fine cornmeal

Add the water to the eggs and beat well. Heat the nut oil to sizzling in a cast-iron skillet. Dip the dandelion blossoms, one at a time, into the egg, and then into the cornmeal. Sauté, turning often, until golden. Drain on brown paper. Serve either hot or cold, as snacks, a vegetable side dish, or a tasty garnish.

*For full, showy blossoms, pick just before using, as blossoms close shortly after picking. The dandelion blossom responds quickly to temperature changes; it opens only in clear weather and bolts as soon as temperatures approach 90° F. Notice the dandelion's yellow-blossoming abundance in spring, its disappearance during the summer, and the return of a few fall flowers as temperatures cool.

WILD RICE WITH HAZELNUTS
AND BLUEBERRIES (serves 12)

2 cups wild rice, washed in cold water
5 cups water
2 wild onions, diced

1 cup shelled dried hazelnuts, diced
1 cup dried blueberries

Combine the rice, water, and onions in a large kettle, bring to a boil, then cover and simmer for approximately 40 minutes, or until most of the water is absorbed. Add the hazelnuts and dried blueberries, mixing thoroughly. Steam, covered, for an additional 20 minutes, stirring occasionally. Serve hot.

SUCCOTASH (serves 8)

1 onion, chopped
1 green pepper, chopped
1 cup water

2 cups shelled lima beans
2 cups yellow corn
2 tablespoons nut butter (see page 9)

Simmer all ingredients together in a large covered kettle for 20 minutes. Serve hot.

This was one of the easiest Indian recipes adopted by the first settlers. The hearty mixture of boiled beans and corn was usually sweetened with bear fat.

LEEKS AND NEW POTATOES (serves 6)

10 whole new potatoes
3 large leeks, quartered
1 teaspoon maple syrup

2 cups water
one 1½-inch cube fatback

Combine all ingredients and simmer, uncovered, until tender, about 25 minutes. Serve hot in bowls with the broth, as a porridge or vegetable.

STEAMED CATTAIL STEMS
(COSSACK ASPARAGUS) (serves 4)

During the spring as the cattails are sprouting upward, before flower stalks emerge, pull upward on the center of the plant, removing the white, syrupy core. Pull 16 stalks. Then remove the outer portion of fronds and cut off the top leaves, saving the inner, white, tender core. This nutritious vegetable is tasty raw, sliced like onions into salad, or eaten alone.

    To cook: Cover the stalks with boiling water and simmer for 10 minutes, or until tender. Serve with nut oil (see page 7) and cider vinegar dressing, or topped with nut butter (see page 9).

    The clear, syrupy juice of this perennial vegetable of the marshlands is an important thickening agent: Added to soups and stews or other vegetable broths, it acts as a "cornstarch." The cattail roots are an important source of starch and carbohydrates.

CATTAILS
Typha latifolia

POKEWEED
Phytolacca americana

BUTTERED POKE SPROUTS (serves 6)

According to Euell Gibbons, poke is "probably the best known and most widely used wild vegetable in America." Poke is best when very young, when the leaves are just unfolding at the top of the sprout. *At its most advanced, mature stages, the leaves, berries, seeds, and large taproot are toxic and can be poisonous.*

Gather, wash, and trim 12 to 16 tender young poke sprouts. Place in a large kettle, cover with the boiling water, and boil for 10 minutes. Pour this cooking water off and discard. Cover the sprouts again with fresh water; add 1 tablespoon wood ashes (see page 4) and 2 cloves wild garlic, some bacon fat (if desired). Simmer slowly. Serve steaming hot, dressed with nut butter (see page 9) or nut oil (see page 7), and cider vinegar to taste.

FRESH CHICKWEED SALAD (serves 8)

2 pounds young chickweed leaves and
   stems
2 teaspoons honey
4 teaspoons sunflower seed butter
   (see page 8)

2 teaspoons sunflower seed oil (see
   page 8)
1/2 cup cider vinegar

Place the washed chickweed in a medium saucepan and cover with boiling water. Simmer, covered, for 3 minutes. Remove from heat and pour off the water. Pour cold water over the greens to set the color and stop the cooking process. Drain at once in a colander.

Combine the remaining ingredients in the bottom of a large salad bowl. Blend to make a smooth dressing. Add the prepared greens. Toss to coat thoroughly, then chill for 1 hour to set the flavor before serving.

By itself, cooked chickweed is a fine addition to fritters, griddle cakes, and any number of dishes. It should be eaten in moderation because of its high nitrate content.

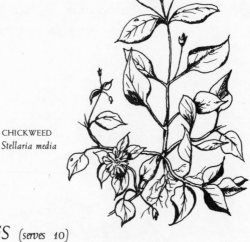

CHICKWEED
Stellaria media

STEWED TOMATOES (serves 10)

3 pounds ripe tomatoes, cored
12 scallions, chopped (including tops)
2 green peppers, chopped
¹/₄ cup water
¹/₄ cup fine cornmeal

¹/₄ cup chopped fresh dillweed
¹/₄ cup chopped fresh basil
1 tablespoon sunflower seed butter (see page 8)

In a covered kettle, simmer the tomatoes, scallions, and peppers in the water for 40 minutes. Stir in the remaining ingredients, mixing thoroughly to break up the softened tomatoes. Simmer for another 10 minutes; serve hot.

BOILED CORN PUDDING (serves 10)

12 large ears corn, shucked
2 quarts water
¹/₄ cup nut butter (see page 9)
1 ¹/₂ cups fine cornmeal

1 tablespoon honey
1 teaspoon chopped fresh parsley
1 egg, beaten

Steam the ears of corn in the water in a large covered kettle for 10 minutes. Remove the corn (reserving the water), cool slightly, then trim the kernels from the cob. (Save and dry the cobs for fire starters.) Reserve the corn in a large bowl.

Mix the nut butter, cornmeal, honey, and parsley together thoroughly. Measure $1/2$ cup hot liquid from the corn pot and beat this into the mixture, then beat in the egg until light. Fold in the corn and mix well. Bring the corn water to a bubbling boil, the drop in the corn pudding batter by tablespoonfuls. Reduce heat and simmer, covered, for 15 minutes; drain and serve as a vegetable. This makes a good potato substitute.

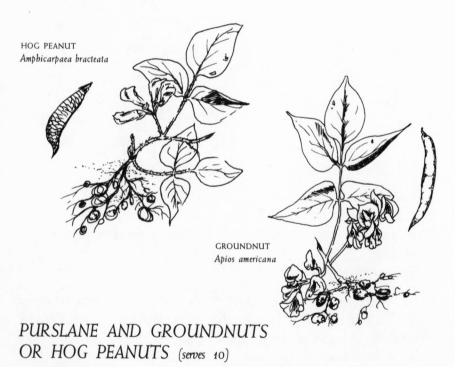

HOG PEANUT
Amphicarpaea bracteata

GROUNDNUT
Apios americana

PURSLANE AND GROUNDNUTS OR HOG PEANUTS (serves 10)

1 quart groundnuts or hog peanuts, washed
1 leek, sliced
3 cups boiling water

1 quart purslane, washed twice
2 small fresh dillweed fronds, chopped
$1/2$ cup sunflower seed butter (see page 8)

In a covered kettle, simmer the groundnuts and leek in the water for 20 minutes. Partially drain. Add the purslane, dill, and sunflower seed butter. Stir and blend thoroughly. Steam for 5 more minutes. Serve hot.

BAKED SWEET POTATOES (serves 6)

6 medium sweet potatoes, scrubbed and
  skins rubbed with nut oil (see
  page 7)

nut butter (see page 9)

Bake the oiled potatoes for 1 hour in a preheated 400° F oven, or in the
ashes of a hot fire (turning to prevent charring). Serve with nut butter.

BAKED PUMPKIN (serves 8)

1 small pumpkin, 12 inches in diameter
2 tablespoons honey
2 tablespoons cider for seasoning

2 tablespoons nut butter (see page 9)
¹/₂ cup cider for basting

Place the whole washed pumpkin in a baking dish in a preheated 350° F
oven for 1¹/₂ hours. Remove, cool, cut a 6-inch-diameter hole in the
top. Remove the pulp and seeds; save the seeds. Remove the pumpkin
meat and mix with the next three ingredients; return to the shell. Replace the pumpkin top and return the pumpkin to the oven to bake,
basting occasionally with additional cider, for 30 minutes more. Serve
the whole pumpkin, scooping out individual portions at the table.

  Toast the reserved seeds on a flat tray in a 350° F oven for 30 minutes and serve as a complement.

BAKED BUTTERNUT SQUASH (serves 8)

2 butternut squash
4 tablespoons nut butter (see page 9)
4 tablespoons honey

4 tablespoons maple syrup
nutmeg and cinnamon or vegetable or
  meat stuffing (optional)

Bake the whole washed squash in a preheated 325° F oven for about 40
minutes, or until the skins wrinkle and are easily pierced, turning once
or twice. (They may be baked in the hot ashes of a fire.) Remove, cool
slightly, cut in half, and scoop out the pulp and seeds. Dot each portion
of squash with a dab of nut butter and drizzle with honey and maple
syrup. (Season lightly with spices, if desired, or stuff with cornmeal,
cooked rice, or meat mixture.) Return to the oven and bake for 30 minutes, or until tender. Serve hot. Toast the seeds on a flat tray in the
same oven for 30 minutes and serve as a complement.

BEANS (*Phaseolus*, various spp.) were as highly regarded as corn by many native Americans. They carefully cultivated and hybridized as many colors as possible. Beans could vary from white and yellow to red and blue, black, magenta, purple, and multicolored. As in the variously colored corn kernels, colored beans signified the six cardinal points: north, south, east, west, zenith, and nadir.

Beans were prepared in a multitude of ways: They were soaked, flattened, and fried into cakes; served cold as salads, or in salads; simmered slowly with meats; made into spicy chilies, stews, soups; and ground and dried as flour. The most colorful varieties were dried and used in games.

BAKED BEANS (BOSTON) (serves 8)

1 pound dried red beans
2 quarts water
¹/₂ pound salt pork, cut into 4 pieces
1 pound dried lima beans
¹/₂ cup molasses

1 teaspoon dried mustard
1 green pepper, diced
4 tablespoons maple sugar
2 onions, quartered
1 cup cider

Place the beans in a large kettle, cover with water, add the salt pork, and simmer, covered, for 2 hours. Add more water as needed. Drain the beans, saving 1 cup of the cooking water. Stir the remaining ingredients into the beans; blend thoroughly.

Pour the beans into a large cooking crock and bake, covered, for 1¹/₂ to 2 hours in a preheated 325° F oven. Just enough liquid should bubble up in the beans and caramelize. Serve hot.

POPCORN (yields about 2 quarts)

¹/₃ cup sunflower seed oil (see page 8)
¹/₂ cup popping corn

¹/₄ cup nut or seed butter (see page 9)
2 cups shelled peanuts

In a saucepan with a lid, heat the oil to the "popping point." Test by dropping in 1 kernel of corn; then add the remainder. With the lid held on securely, shake the pan until the corn stops popping. Pour immediately into a large bowl. Place the nut (or seed) butter and the peanuts in the still-warm pan and return to the heat to melt the butter and lightly coat the nuts. Toast and stir. Then pour over the popcorn and serve.

SQUASH VINE AND BLOSSOMS
Cucurbitaceae family

FRIED SQUASH (OR PUMPKIN) BLOSSOMS *(serves 8)*

1 cup milk
1 egg
1 tablespoon flour
1 teaspoon ground dried sassafras leaves
3 dozen male blossoms,* picked just
    before they open, mashed

½ cup oil
garnish: chopped fresh mint leaves or
    dillweed

Blend the milk, egg, flour, and seasoning in a bowl with a fork. Beat the batter until smooth. Place the mashed blossoms in the batter, stir gently, and allow to soak for 10 minutes. Heat the oil in a cast-iron skillet until hot. Fry the batter-coated blossoms, a few at a time, until golden, turning once. Drain on brown paper. Serve hot, garnished with mint leaves or dill.

*The male blossoms are the larger, infertile blossoms without an ovary (the swelling at the base of the flower).

REED GRASS (*Phragmites communis*) is one of the tallest marsh plants in North America. This perennial grass, introduced from Eurasia, played a vital role in the lives of the American Indians, as well as the colonists. The tall aerial parts of the Common Reed were used for arrow shafts, weaving, thatching, mats, and insulation; the seeds were a grain source for gruels, cereals, and breads; the early shoots were fine as a raw or cooked vegetable; and the roots and rhizomes, an excellent sugar source, were dug and roasted year-round.

PHRAGMITES GRUEL (serves 2)

½ cup phragmites seeds   maple syrup or nut milk (see page 7)
3 wintergreen berries   to taste
2 cups boiling water

Collect 12 to 15 seed heads of the phragmites (in late summer or autumn). Remove the tiny seeds by hand, and crush (hulls and all) with the wintergreen berries for flavor. Add to the boiling water in a medium saucepan, cover, and cook slowly until it becomes a thin, red mixture — about 30 minutes. Sweeten with maple syrup or nut milk if desired, or simply enjoy this nutritious, whole-grain cereal by itself.

ARROWHEAD, Duck Potato, Wapato, Katniss (*Sagittaria latifolia*), is a prodigious aquatic plant that was a staple food of the American Indians all across our continent. One of our most valuable native foods, arrowhead roots are delectable and nutritious, resembling new potatoes. They can be eaten raw, though they contain a bitter, milky juice that becomes sweet and tasty when the tubers are dried or cooked. Prepare these wild tubers exactly like potatoes. Dried and ground into flour, they are useful in many other food forms.

REED GRASS
Phragmites communis

CARAMELIZED ARROWHEAD TUBERS (serves 6 to 8)

25 egg-sized arrowhead tubers   *8 tablespoons sunflour seed butter*
¹/₂ cup maple syrup   *(see page 8)*

Clean the tubers and boil them (unpeeled) in a covered pot for 20 minutes or until soft. Cool and peel. Heat the maple syrup in a heavy skillet over low heat, cooking slowly so as not to burn, until it is golden brown. Stir in the sunflower seed butter and blend well. Add the tubers, rolling to coat them well. Serve hot.

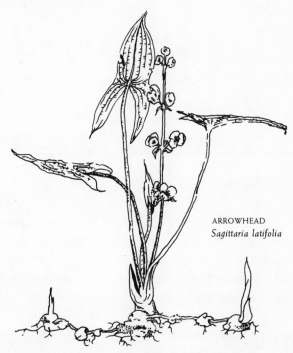

ARROWHEAD
Sagittaria latifolia

SOLOMON'S SEAL or Sealwort (*Polygonatum pubescens*). This herb is found in profusion in rich, shaded woods. Many of the New England tribes dried the spring-harvested shoots for future needs; they later taught the French and English colonists to do the same. The macerated roots and rhizomes were valued as an astringent and diuretic tonic. The Iroquois also used the thick rootstocks to pound into breads and ate the tender young shoots as spring greens and food extenders.

FALSE SOLOMON'S SEAL, False Spikenard, Scurvyberries (*Smilacina racemosa*). A widespread and graceful woodland plant favoring shaded woods and moist environments, false Solomon's seal provides a healthful and re-

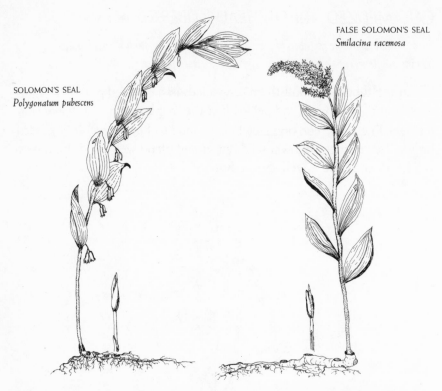

SOLOMON'S SEAL
Polygonatum pubescens

FALSE SOLOMON'S SEAL
Smilacina racemosa

freshing trailside nibble. The Indians used the entire plant throughout its growing season. The young shoots may be enjoyed as steamed asparagus in early spring; the young leaves, before blossomtime, are excellent in raw salads or lightly steamed as a potherb; the aromatic and starchy rootstocks may be cooked like potatoes or pickled. (To rid the rootstocks of their bitter taste, they should first be soaked for several hours in water and wood ashes, then rinsed and boiled in fresh water for 30 minutes to eliminate the lye.)

INDIAN CUCUMBER or Cucumber Root (*Medeola virginiana*) is a slender, perennial woodland herb and a delicious vegetable. It is principally sought for its crisp, starchy rootstock, which has the delicate taste of cucumber. Enjoyed raw in salads, as a lone vegetable, or pickled, this plant was used by numerous tribes. Harvest sparingly and only when found growing in abundance.

There are many plants native to this continent but not necessarily acclimatized to the Northeast that cannot be overlooked. Their importance to us in the twentieth century is heightened when we reflect on their centuries of usefulness to the Amerindians.

PRICKLY PEAR, Indian Fig, Beavertail, Devil's Tongue, Tuna (*Opuntia vulgaris* and var. spp.). These common broad-leafed spiny cacti are hardy and acclimatized from coast to coast. The fruits that form after the showy yellow blossoms were enjoyed in many cultures; they are still seasonal favorites in many parts of the country and are high in calcium. They are enjoyed fresh in salads, chopped in omelettes and stews, and in juices, jellies, and pickles.

NIGHT-BLOOMING CEREUS, Deerhorn Cactus, Christ-in-the-cradle, Reina de la Noche (*Peniocereus greggii*). This huge, plain cactus is cultivated today essentially for its large, showy white blossoms with special fragrance that open only after sundown, each for one night's duration. Across most of the Southwest to Mexico, this rangy plant is found growing among the creosote shrubs. The Amerindians dug these large roots to bake or boil as a starchy vegetable.

NIGHT-BLOOMING CEREUS BLOSSOM
Peniocereus greggii

JOJOBA, Coffee Bush, Wild Hazel, Goat Nut, Deer Nut (*Simmondsia californica*). This southern evergreen shrub favors dry, coarse desert soils, and as a native botanical cultivar of the southern tribes it has an impressive number of uses. This leathery-leafed bush produces acornlike nuts that have been food, medicine, and beverage material for the Amerindians for centuries. These fruits are almost 50 percent oil, and this oil is of enormous commercial value.

Botanical Charts

Caution: A few of these plants might be found growing in the company of toxic near-look-alikes. Do not mistake any other wild lilies for the edible daylily, and do not mistake the poisonous dogbane for milkweed.

Never take all of the plants growing in one area.

Key: *Harvesttime:*   *Usage*
        Sp = *Spring*   F = *Food*
        S = *Summer*   T = *Technology*
        F = *Fall*   C = *Charm*
        W = *Winter*   D = *Dye*
                     B = *Beverage*
                     M = *Medicine*

Note: All season here refers to the typical growing seasons of these particular plants, which vary across the country. The plant parts dictate their own harvesttime.

I. Wild Vegetables and Flavorings (Raw)

These plants are delightful additions to salads and delicious to eat or nibble without cooking. Remember that their nutritive value is at its maximum when they are eaten very shortly after picking.

Plant	Plant Part Used	Usage	Harvesttime
1. Barberry	leaves, berries	M, B, D, F	Sp
2. Blackberry	shoots & leaves	M, B, F	All year
3. Brooklime	leaves, stems	M, F	Sp, S
4. Burdock	leaves, leaf stalks	F	Sp, S
5. Calamus	shoots	M, F	Sp
6. Catbrier	shoots, leaves	B, F	Sp, S
7. Cattail	shoots, stems, pollen	T, B, F	Sp, S
8. Chickweed	leaves	F	Sp, S, F
9. Chicory	leaves	B, F	Sp
10. Chive, Wild	leaves	M, F	All season
11. Cleavers	shoots	T, B, F	Sp
12. Clover	leaves, blossoms	M, B, F	All season
13. Coriander	leaves, seeds	F	All season
14. Dandelion	leaves, blossoms	M, B, F	Sp
15. Daylily	tubers, blossoms	F	All season
16. Dewberry	shoots, leaves	M, B	Sp, S
17. Dill	leaves, seeds	M, F	All season
18. Garlic, Wild	leaves, bulbs	M, F	All year
19. Great Bulrush	shoots, pollen	T, F	Sp, S

Plant	Plant Part Used	Usage	Harvesttime
20. Horseradish	young leaves	M, F	Sp
21. Indian Cucumber	roots	F	All season
22. Jerusalem Artichoke	tubers	F	F
23. Lamb's Quarters	leaves, seeds	F	All season
24. Leek, Wild	bulbs, leaves	F	Sp
25. Milkweed	young sprouts	T, M	Sp
26. Mint, Wild	leaves	C, M, B, F	All season
27. Mustard, Wild Black	leaves	F	Sp
28. Nasturtium	leaves, buds, blossoms	F	All season
29. Onion, Wild	bulbs, greens	M, D, F	All season
30. Pasture Brake Fern	fiddlehead	C, F	Early Sp
31. Pennyroyal	leaves	M, B, F	All season
32. Purslane	leaves, stalks	F	All season
33. Raspberry	shoots, leaves	M, B, F	All season
34. Rose	blossoms, hips	C, M, B, F	All season
35. Sheep Sorrel	leaves	F	Sp
36. Shepherd's Purse	leaves	F	Sp, S
37. Thistle	leaves	T, F	Sp
38. Violet	leaves, blossoms	M, F	Sp, S
39. Watercress	leaves, shoots	F	All season
40. Winter Cress	leaves, shoots	F	All season
41. Wood Sorrel	leaves, blossoms	F	All season

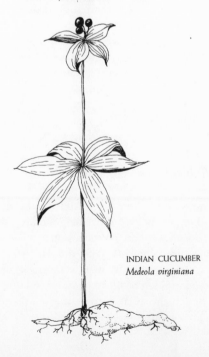

INDIAN CUCUMBER
Medeola virginiana

II. Wild Vegetables (Steamed)

The shoots, leaves, and plant parts of these wild potherbs should be served like spinach or asparagus. The young leaves and shoots at the tops of the stems are the mildest and tenderest. These should be rinsed in cold water and steamed in a minimum of plain or lightly seasoned water. *Do not overcook.* These are delicious dressed with natural vinegars and nut oils or butters.

Plant	Plant Part Used	Harvesttime
1. Bracken Fern	fiddlehead	Early Sp
2. Brooklime	leaves, stems	Sp, S
3. Catbrier	leaves, stems	Sp, S
4. Cattail	shoots, flowers	Sp, S
5. Chickweed	whole plant	Sp, S
6. Cleavers	shoots	Sp
7. Coltsfoot	leaves	Sp, S
8. Dandelion	leaves, buds	Sp
9. Daylily	buds, blossoms, tubers	All season
10. Ferns	fiddleheads	Early Sp
11. Green Amaranth	leaves, shoots	Sp, S
12. Horseradish	young leaves	Sp
13. Lamb's Quarters	leaves, shoots	All season
14. Milkweed	buds, blossoms, tiny pods	Sp, S
15. Mint	leaves, buds	All season
16. Plantain	young leaves	Sp
17. Purslane	leaves, shoots, stems	All season
18. Sheep Sorrel	leaves	Until late S
19. Thistle	leaves, stems (stripped)	Sp, S
20. Violet	blossoms, leaves	Sp
21. Watercress	leaves, shoots	All year
22. Wild Onion	bulbs, greens	All season

III. Wild Vegetables (Well Cooked)

Certain plants require more preparation and should be cooked in two or more changes of water. Longer cooking times help modify their bitterness or stronger flavor. Some botanicals contain poisonous substances that are soluble in the cooking water, destroyed by heat, and thrown away in the necessary water changes. Tougher, stringier plants, such as burdock, chicory and poke, can be tenderized by adding a pinch of bicarbonate of soda (or wood ashes) to the *first* cooking water. Though the vitamin content is minimized by such preparations, essential minerals do remain.

Plant	Plant Part Used	Harvesttime
1. Burdock	roots, stems, leaves	Sp, S
2. Chicory	leaves	Sp
3. Dandelion	roots, leaves	S
4. Jewelweed	shoots, leaves	Early Sp
5. Mallow	leaves, fruits	Sp, S
6. Marsh Marigold	leaves	Sp
7. Milkweed	shoots	Early Sp
8. Mustard	leaves	Sp
9. Nettle	tops, leaves	Sp, S
10. Ostrich Fern	fiddlehead	Early Sp
11. Pokeweed	shoots, leaves	Early Sp
12. Salsify	roots, leaves	All season
13. Shepherd's Purse	leaves	Sp, S
14. Winter Cress	leaves, stalks	All year

BURDOCK
Arctium lappa

IV. Natural Flours and Flour Extenders

Any of the following botanicals may be dehydrated and ground to make flour. The tastiest and most nutritious wild flours are those prepared from nutmeats. Seeds of the various botanicals can easily be used to make flour as well as cereals, gruels, and puddings.

The finest flour in nature, which needs no sifting or refining, is cattail and bulrush pollen. However, its fineness also makes it very hard to wet, so it is easier to mix the pollen with a greater portion of other flour.

Plant	Plant Part Used	Harvesttime
1. Acorn	nutmeats	F, S
2. Arrowhead	tubers	F, S
3. Beech	nuts	F
4. Black Walnuts	nuts	F
5. Butternut	nuts	F
6. Cattail	roots, pollen	All year (midsummer)
7. Corn	seeds	S, F
8. Daylily	tubers	S, F
9. Dock	seeds	F
10. Great Bulrush	roots, pollen, seeds	S, F
11. Green Amaranth	seeds	S, F
12. Groundnuts	tubers	S, F
13. Hazelnuts	nuts	F
14. Hickory	nuts	F
15. Jerusalem Artichoke	tubers	F
16. Lamb's Quarters	seeds	F
17. Potato	tubers	F
18. Purslane	seeds	F
19. Shepherd's Purse	seeds	F
20. Sunflower	seeds	F
21. Wild Leek	bulbs, greens	Sp
22. Wild Rice	seeds	F
23. Yellow Pond Lily	tubers	F

IV

NATIVE FERNS, LICHENS, AND MOSSES

BRACKEN FERN
Pteridium aquilinum

Ferns

One of the first green edible plants in spring is the newly emerging
fiddleheads (curled crosiers) of ferns. High in oil and starch, this fine
delicate vegetable is always best picked early in the day while fresh-fla-
vored and when the long-stemmed crosiers snap crisply in your hand.
The same fronds would be overgrown by afternoon. In New England,
the fiddlehead season lasts only about 3 weeks in May, depending on
the weather.

The Indians used more than twenty species of indigenous ferns as
food. In early spring the new fiddleheads were gathered and enjoyed
raw or cooked as a vegetable or simmered in soups and stews for their
thickening qualities. Brought to a boil and then simmered for 30 minutes, the young, slender stalks can be seasoned and served as a delectable asparaguslike vegetable. The rhizomes are also an important
food source: Roasted or baked, then ground Indian fashion, the fern
roots can be worked with other substances into cakes or gruels, or

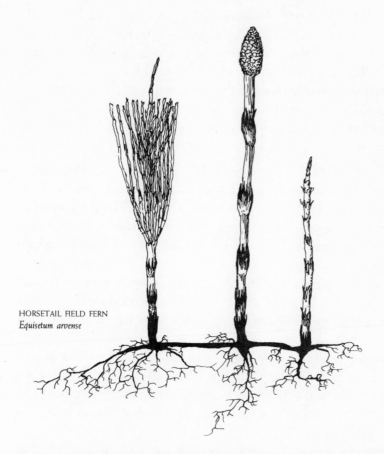

HORSETAIL FIELD FERN
Equisetum arvense

dried and used as flour for breads. The rhizomes of bracken are best utilized this way. The older, full-grown fronds of most species are slightly toxic and inedible. Grazing animals have been poisoned by eating too many fern fronds.

Never harvest more than half of the fiddleheads from any cluster!

BRACKEN, Pasture Brake, Eagle Fern (*Pteridium aquilinum*). This is our common, most widespread fern, rising singly from long, slender rhizomes in dry, sandy soils. The small fiddleheads are distinctly three-forked, easily picked and cleaned, and delicious raw, especially in salads. Lightly steamed, these fiddleheads are excellent pickled or used with other vegetables. The Indians pounded the rootstocks into flour for bread. *Caution:* The raw plant contains an enzyme that can destroy vitamin B_1 (thiamine). Do not eat it in large quantities.

CINNAMON FERN *(Osmunda cinnamomea)*. This tall, graceful fern of the swamps and moist woodlands was gathered as a favored spring potherb by many East Coast tribes for their soups and meat stews. Gather when about 8 inches tall; the crosier plus 2 inches of stem are desirable. Thoroughly wash and remove the bronze woolly covering (used by the Indians as an absorbent dressing for open sores and wounds). This species of fiddlehead is somewhat dry in texture and needs complementary seasonings.

HORSETAIL FIELD FERN, Scouring Rush, Shave Brush, Pewterwort, Mare's Tail *(Equisetum arvense* and 2 spp.). These dwarf survivors of the carboniferous woodlands seem to thrive in any soil. Three major tribes record distinct food usage of this fern. The Hopis dried and ground the stems with cornmeal and ate the mixture as gruel or baked it into a pone bread.

The stems contain silica, and the plant structure is abrasive enough to make this an excellent pot scrubber and equally good for brightening gunstocks and pewter. An interesting yellow-gray dye is created from the stalks.

As a spring food the young emerging stalks can be treated like asparagus. They are a rather pallid but mineral-rich early vegetable, known to be toxic and poisonous in sufficient amounts to livestock. The bitter taste of this wilderness food is removed when boiled in two to three changes of water.

Perhaps the horsetail's most beneficial use is as an astringent to wash and stop the bleeding of external wounds. Thus, a decoction made from boiling the stems into a body lotion is possibly their best recipe.

OSTRICH FERN *(Matteuccia struthiopteris)*. One of our largest ferns and very common in the East, the ostrich fern favors the rich, alluvial soil of river and stream banks and swamps. Two or three fern clusters can supply enough fiddleheads for a meal; *no more than half of the emerging crosiers are required.* These large, easy-to-clean fiddleheads may be enjoyed raw in salads or slightly steamed for 10 minutes.

SENSITIVE FERN, Bead Fern *(Onoclea sensibilis)*. This widespread common fern favors damp environments. The prolific pale reddish-green fiddleheads were spring favorites of the Iroquois, who also gathered and ate the rhizomes in lean times. The classic beaded fertile frond is this fern's hallmark. These beaded fronds are attractive in dried harvest arrangements.

SALSIFY
Tragopogon porrifolius

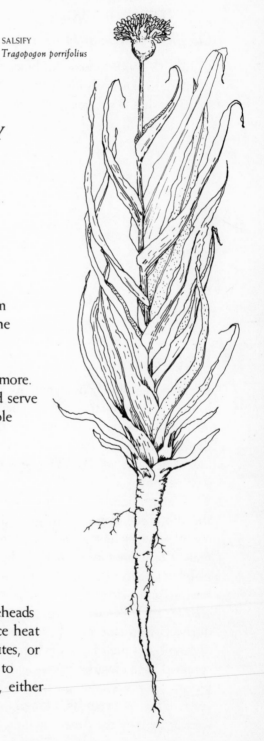

FIDDLEHEADS AND SALSIFY ROOTS (serves 6 to 8)

2 dozen salsify roots, peeled
½ cup boiling water
4 dozen ostrich fiddleheads
1 tablespoon cider vinegar
1 tablespoon sunflower seed oil (see
   page 8)

Place the salsify roots in a medium
pot. Cover with the water; add the
fiddleheads and the remaining
ingredients, and stir thoroughly.
Simmer, covered, for 10 minutes more.
Serve hot, or marinate further and serve
cold. A tasty and exciting vegetable
combination!

FIDDLEHEAD STEW (serves 8)

4 dozen fiddleheads
2 cups boiling water
1 teaspoon nut oil (see page 7)
½ cup nut butter (see page 9)

In a medium pot, cover the fiddleheads
with the water and nut oil. Reduce heat
and simmer, covered, for 20 minutes, or
until tender. Top with nut butter to
enhance the flavor, and serve hot, either
alone or on a nest of wild rice or
cornmeal (grits).

ROASTED RHIZOMES
OF BRACKEN FERN (serves 6)

Gather 18 good rhizomes of bracken; scrub, wash, and peel. Bake like potatoes in hot coals for 30 minutes. Serve hot. Virginia Indians used hickory ashes as seasonings for these wild vegetables.

ICELAND MOSS
Cetraria islandica

Lichens

Many species of lichens contain rock-dissolving bitter acids, which tend to be cathartic to the system when ingested. To lessen this cathartic quality somewhat and to enhance the edibility of certain species, soak the lichens for several hours or overnight. Change the water three or four times and add 1 tablespoon wood ashes (see page 4) or baking soda per pot.

Though lichens appear rather drab, dry, and forbidding, growing as they do in seemingly sterile ground or on rocks and tree barks, several notable species have been important survival foods for people and animals. Contemporary evidence indicates that the "manna from heaven" of biblical accounts was a form of lichen blown free from its rocky habitats and swirled into the valleys. Two species, *Lecanora affinis* and *L. esculenta,* are still eaten by desert tribes, and records confirm the extraordinary circumstances of these lichens providing food for large numbers of people and their herds of sheep or cattle. This type of occurrence has repeated itself at various times and in diverse areas throughout recorded history; at times large areas have been covered with a grayish-white layer of bitter, irregular "clumps," from 3 to 6 inches thick. Lichens were utilized by the American Indians throughout prehistory.

Lichens have various medicinal properties that have proved beneficial to many Indian tribes, and as a noteworthy dye base the lichens have produced dozens of lovely soft colors.

ICELAND MOSS (*Cetraria islandica*). A common northern lichen, Iceland moss is found growing in broad-cushioned mats of olive green to purple, which pale to gray as they dry. The paper-thin branching growth prefers sandy soil and colder, more exposed terrain. It has long been sought as a medicinal and nutritive tonic to relieve bronchial problems. This lichen contains a large amount of starch, which is soluble in boiling water and gelatinizes on cooling. Aside from its nutritive value it improves both the appetite and digestion.

Iceland moss is used as flour and in soups, puddings, blancmange, and medicines.

ICELAND MOSS JELLY

Gather 2 cups Iceland moss and wash. Place in a pot, cover with 2 cups boiling water, cover the pot, and let stand for 3 hours. Stir, strain, and sweeten to taste with honey or maple syrup. Up to 1 pound fresh wild berries or ½ cup citrus peel may be added. For children, the jelly may be boiled briefly in milk for greater palatability.

REINDEER MOSS (*Cladonia rangiferina* and spp.) is another common northern lichen forming large irregular carpets on sandy ground. The antler-like branchlets of silvery gray are hollow; they are rubbery and spongy when wet and brittle when dry. This appealing lichen has had many noteworthy uses since prerecorded time in soups, gruels, and blancmange. In a dried, powdered form it may be used like cornstarch and baked as bread.

Northern Indian tribes depended upon this food source for their winter survival. Caribou and reindeer continue to do so.

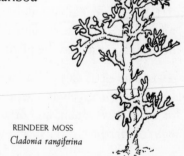

REINDEER MOSS
Cladonia rangiferina

CLUB-MOSS
Lycopodium clavatum

Mosses

CLUB-MOSSES (*Lycopodiaceae* family). This is one of the oldest plant groups, dating back perhaps three hundred million years. These dwarf spore-producing evergreens perennially spread by running rootstocks in dense woodland carpets. Many club-mosses have erect spore-bearing structures, which produce water-resistant spores. These have been used as dusting powder to prevent skin chafing, to treat eczema, and especially to dust on open wounds. High flammable, the spores have also been used in small fireworks and in photographic flashes.

Considered inedible, the club-mosses have significant medicinal and technological benefits. They seem to mirror the appearance of the pines, hemlocks, and cedars they so often grow beneath. Of the more than one hundred species, the most common North American ones are profiled here.

CLUB-MOSS, Vegetable Sulphur, Wolf's Claw, Stag's Horn Moss (*Lycopodium clavatum*). The Indians inhaled the yellowish spores to stop nosebleed and considered the plant a diuretic.

CHRISTMAS CLUB-MOSS, Running Cedar, Ground Pine (*Lycopodium complanatum*). Pale green and delicately spreading, this species was collected for decorative roping and ornamentation and was used as well in treatment of diarrhea, dropsy, and scurvy.

FIR CLUB-MOSS or Mountain Club-moss *(Lycopodium selago)*. A northern mountain species used medicinally as an emetic and sedative, and externally as an insect repellent on animals.

TREE CLUB-MOSS or Princess Pine *(Lycopodium obscurum)* is a multibranched miniature pine tree in appearance. The stems and leaves were used as mordants to fix dyes in woolens.

V

❧

WILD
MUSHROOMS

$\mathbf{T}$he fungi are unique and powerful plants in all their various forms: mushrooms, molds, blights, and rusts. They can feed and cure us, as well as induce visions and kill us. Those that are safe to eat make a nutritious and delectable vegetable group and are sought for their many flavors and textures. They are a fine addition to any meal, year-round. Wild mushrooms are rich in folic acid and are a particularly good source of B vitamins; when mushrooms are grown in light, vitamin D becomes quite abundant. Because some fungi are deadly, only a favored few are profiled here. Many edible varieties were eaten raw or cooked by the American Indians.

As a precaution, the beginner should avoid all wild mushrooms until proper identification can be made.

1. Start with a simple list of species and an excellent mushroom guide. *Identify carefully and thoroughly!*
2. When collecting several species at a time, *keep each type separate.* One poisonous Amanita can make the entire batch of edible species deadly.
3. Use only fresh, healthy mushrooms in order to avoid food poisoning. If you can't use them right away, they may be stored in an uncovered container in the refrigerator for up to 24 hours.
4. You might be allergic to some species. Even though a new mushroom seems absolutely delectable, eat only a small portion (no more than ¼ cup) and wait at least 24 hours to be sure there are no side effects. When first trying a new mushroom, sauté in nut butter (see page 9) or scramble with an egg to savor its flavor.

COMMON MOREL
Morchella esculenta

COMMON MOREL or Sponge Morel (*Morchella esculenta*); BLACK MOREL (*M. augusticeps*). The deeply pitted spongelike cap is fused to the stem at the lower end (unlike the poisonous false morels, whose caps hang skirtlike around the stem). Favoring orchards, moist woods, and especially burned fields, the common morel is found throughout the northeastern United States. It is most common in May after heavy spring rains. The pale tan to grayish cap is oval to cone-shaped, and the entire growth is hollow inside. The stem is tall, stout, creamy, and often furrowed. Excellent stuffed or cut in long slices and sautéed briefly in nut oil (see page 7).

FAIRY RING MUSHROOM (*Marasmius oreades*) is a small, cap-shaped mushroom, white to pale yellow-brown, on a slender stem. The cap is broad, smooth, and moist; the flesh is thick and creamy pink to tan; the gills are broad and creamy white; the stem is long. Common in grassy areas where it often forms neat circles, it may be gathered June to September throughout most of the United States. It is quite a popular vegetable, with a delicious taste and fragrance. Fairy ring caps have a very choice flavor and dry well for preservation as distinctive food additives. Enjoy careful harvesting when this delectable species is found, and with proper irrigation the same area will produce mushrooms all summer.

MEADOW MUSHROOMS (*Agaricus campestris, A. arvensis*). The most common mushroom found in open pastures and lawns, the meadow mushroom is *never found in the woods*. These short, white to brown mushrooms were enjoyed by numerous tribes. The cap surface is silky and dry; the flesh is soft white to pale pink; the gills are free and crowded; the stem is short.

This species is a close relative to the commercially grown mushroom, and the flavor is similar. They may be collected June through October, although like most wild mushrooms they are best in late summer with the early fall rains. Excellent raw, marinated, or sautéed with eggs or rice.

MEADOW MUSHROOM
Agaricus campestris

OYSTER MUSHROOM (*Pleurotus ostreatus*). The delicious oyster-gray convex cap may be gathered through late fall into December in the Northeast, though the earlier, younger mushrooms are the most tender. Found in clusters attached to deciduous trees (usually elm, oak, beech, birch, or maple), these mushrooms have lilac spores, white, broad, radiating gills, and almost no stem. ANGEL WINGS (*Pleurotus porrigens*) are very similar to oyster mushrooms and are found in the same places; their caps and spores are white. Excellent sautéed or in stews, both mushrooms taste much like scrambled eggs.

OYSTER MUSHROOM
Pleurotus ostreatus

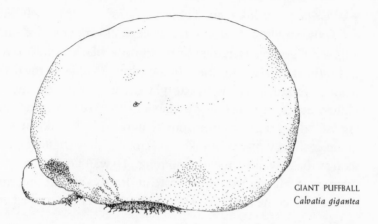

GIANT PUFFBALL
Calvatia gigantea

PUFFBALLS, Giant (*Calvatia gigantea*), are large, usually smooth, balloon-shaped mushrooms growing directly from the ground. Eight to fifteen inches in diameter and white when young, puffballs are found in the rich, disturbed soil of barnyards, pastures, and lawns. They grow singly or in clusters throughout the United States. *Warning:* Be sure the interior flesh is *pure white*, indicating it is fresh; if yellowish, the mushroom will be bitter. Discard if the inside shows a shadowy mushroom form or gills, which indicate that it may be the poisonous Amanita.*

Zunis gathered great quantities of puffballs to eat fresh or to dry for the winter. Many tribes cut this species into chunks and fried it like meat. All puffballs are edible in the young stage while the flesh is white; peel before cooking and prepare as you would cultivated mushrooms. Puffballs are one of the safest groups of fungi to harvest; one genus, *Scleroderma*, may cause slight sickness.

Some additional family members are: SKULL-SHAPED PUFFBALL (*Calvatia craniiformis*), PAPERY PUFFBALL (*Bovista pila*), CUP-SHAPED PUFFBALL (*Calvatia cynthiformis*), GEMMED PUFFBALL (*Lycoperdon perlatum*).

EDIBLE PUFFBALL

IMMATURE
POISONOUS AMANITA

*See the Reference Guide for suitable mushroom guidebooks. *Foraging for Wild Edible Mushrooms,* by Karen and Richard Haard, is especially useful.

SHAGGY MANE or Ink Cap (*Coprinus comatus*). When newly formed, this delicious, prolific mushroom resembles a closed, shingled umbrella and ing, self-digesting enzymes turn it into a black, inky mess. When a scaly; the flesh is white; the gills are white, free, and crowded; the stem is long. Found in lawns, waste places, and roadsides throughout the United States, it is a showy member of the ink cap group; upon ripening, self-digesting enzymes turn it into a black, inky mess. When a group of shaggy manes or ink caps is found, they should be harvested as soon as the dew dries in early morning. To wait until evening on a warm summer or fall day would be wasteful, for the mushrooms are likely to ripen and become inedible. They make an excellent cooked vegetable.

SULPHUR SHELF (*Polyporus sulphureus*) and CHICKEN-OF-THE-WOODS (*Laetiporus sulphureus*) are found in dry, open woods, throughout North America, on dead or injured deciduous trees. They grow in large, many-leveled yellow to orange brackets (shelves) with tiny pores on the underside. The cap is yellow to orange, broad, smooth, and fluted; the flesh is white; the pores are a sulphur-yellow. Harvest the tender outer portions in late summer and early fall. This mushroom is one of the finest edible mushrooms. Requiring longer cooking than most, this firm-textured species has the consistency of chicken breast meat when sliced and sautéed or simmered for 30 minutes. Excellent in potages and casseroles.

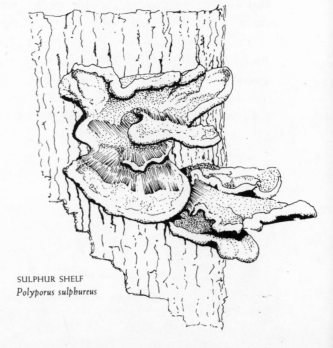

SULPHUR SHELF
Polyporus sulphureus

Cooking Wild Mushrooms

Preparation begins in the field with clean collecting habits. Brush off any dirt or debris and avoid wetting or mixing collections. Remember that *water is an enemy of most mushrooms,* so wash only when truly necessary. Because mushrooms deteriorate rapidly, they should be cleaned and parboiled as soon as possible after collection.

For best natural flavor and texture, never overcook or overspice mushrooms. Indeed, the raw mushroom retains a delicate flavor and aroma that often change or dissipate in cooking.

An excellent use of raw sliced mushrooms is in a savory wild-salad bowl. A natural next step is to marinate the fresh mushrooms. *If they are left covered and at room temperature,* the deterioration of the wild mushrooms by bacteria may quickly lead to food poisoning.

MARINATED MUSHROOMS AND WILD LEEKS (serves 8 to 10)

4 cups fresh, firm mushrooms (shaggy manes, meadow mushrooms, etc.)
2 cups wild leek bulbs
1/2 cup cider vinegar
1/2 cup sunflower seed oil (see page 8)
1 tablespoon chopped fresh parsley
1 teaspoon dillseed

Simmer the mushrooms and leeks in a small amount of boiling water for 5 minutes. Drain, cool, and place in a crock or glass jar. Cover with the remaining ingredients blended into a sauce and store in the refrigerator, loosely covered, for 24 hours or more before serving.

PICKLED MUSHROOMS (serves 8 to 10)

1 cup water
1 cup cider vinegar
1 teaspoon coltsfoot ashes, optional (see page 27)
1 small onion, diced
1 teaspoon crumbled dried bayberry leaves
1 tablespoon favored pickling spices
4 cups steamed wild mushrooms, drained (use about 6 cups raw mushrooms)

Combine all ingredients (except the mushrooms) and simmer, covered, for 5 minutes. Remove from heat and cool. Place the mushrooms in a large glass jar and strain the pickling broth over them; cover the jar and refrigerate for 24 hours or more before serving. These should keep safely in the refrigerator for days.

SAUTÉED MUSHROOMS (serves 8 to 10)

4 tablespoons nut oil (see page 7) or nut butter (see page 9)

2 teaspoons lemon juice

½ teaspoon coltsfoot ashes, optional (see page 27)

½ teaspoon chopped fresh wild marjoram

½ teaspoon wild mustard seeds

5 cups fresh mushrooms, sliced

Warm the nut oil (or nut butter) and lemon juice in a broad cast-iron skillet. Add the remaining ingredients and sauté over medium heat for barely 5 minutes, or until tender. Serve warm to complement any meal.

MEADOW MUSHROOM PIE (serves 8 to 10)

3 cups fresh meadow mushrooms, chopped

3 tablespoons nut butter (see page 9)

1 egg, beaten

4 cups mashed potatoes

2 tablespoons chopped fresh dillweed

1 tablespoon coltsfoot ashes, optional (see page 27)

1 tablespoon chopped fresh parsley

1 tablespoon chopped onion

½ cup water

¼ cup fine cornmeal

Sauté the mushrooms in the nut butter until golden — about 5 minutes. Combine the egg and mashed potato and press to cover the bottom and sides of a deep baking dish evenly. Blend 1 tablespoon of the dill, the coltsfoot ashes, the parsley, the onion, and the water with the mushrooms and gently turn the mixture into the potato crust. Sprinkle the top with the cornmeal and additional dill. Bake in a preheated 375° F oven for 30 minutes. Serve hot.

SHAGGY MANE
Coprinus comatus

SHAGGY MANE PIE (serves 6 to 8)

4 cups large fresh shaggy manes, caps
    only
4 cups fine cornmeal
1 cup cattail flour (see page 66)

2 tablespoons chopped fresh chives
$^{1}/_{4}$ cup nut oil (see page 7)
4 eggs, beaten

Cut the mushroom caps into $^{1}/_{2}$-inch slices, place in a pot, and almost cover with water. Bring to a boil and simmer, covered, for 10 minutes. Remove from heat and cool in the broth. Mix together the cornmeal, cattail flour, and chives. Grease a glass baking dish or crock with some of the nut oil and alternately layer the mushrooms with the flour mixture. Cover with the eggs, drizzle the remaining nut oil over the top, and bake in a preheated 375° F oven until set — about 40 minutes.

Preserving Wild Mushrooms

Although many mushroom enthusiasts follow the "black bear" approach of eating fresh mushrooms in abundance, wild mushrooms may be kept by freezing, canning, and drying. The latter is the simplest method and is especially good for those species put by for use in soups, gravies, casseroles, and sauces.

Do not wash mushrooms that will be dried. Brush off the dirt and trim; large ones should be cut in half and sliced into $^{1}/_{2}$-inch segments, or you may chop them. Spread the pieces to dry away from sunlight in any clean, ventilated setting. Keep the pieces from touching (as you would any herbs and fruits in the drying process).

VI

❧

WILD
MEATS

It is essential that wild game be prepared properly for cooking. The animal should be cleaned immediately, or the meat might absorb a bad flavor from the last meal ingested.

The animal should be hung in a cool place and enclosed in a cheesecloth bag to protect it from flies. Small animals and birds should hang for 48 hours in order for body heat to dissipate.

If not needed immediately, small game may be frozen in cartons or bags of water with a little vinegar. This protects the meat from freezer burn and makes it juicier and more tender. With defrosting, this marinade melts away; if it was lightly spiced in advance, it can be reserved to begin the preparation process.

Most eastern tribes enjoyed only one full meal a day, a combination of breakfast and lunch, which they ate before noon. This was the time for hearty food, a robust rack of game or broiled fish, a crisp salad, baked pumpkin or squash, crunchy hazelnut cakes. The men ate first, usually from wooden or earthenware bowls. Afterward, the women and children ate what was left.

John Bartram visited the Iroquois in 1743 and described a feast he was served: "This repast consisted of three great kettles of Indian corn soup, or thin hominy, with dry'd eels and other fish boiled in it, and one kettle full of young squashes and their flowers boiled in water, and a little meal mixed . . . last of all was served a great bowl full of Indian dumplings, made of new, soft corn, cut or scraped off the ear, then with the addition of some boiled beans, lapped well up in Indian corn leaves, this is good hearty provision."*

BRUNSWICK STEW (serves 12 to 14)

The Jamestown settlers gave the name to this particularly favorite "game soup" prepared by the women of the Powhatan, Cherokee, and Chickahominy tribes. The seasonal mixture of game or fowl was usually squirrel, rabbit, or turkey accompanied by corn, beans, and tomatoes. It is a grand way of absorbing leftovers.

one 5-pound capon or boiling chicken	2 cups shelled lima beans
2 dried bayberry leaves	10 dried juniper berries
3 sprigs parsley	1/2 teaspoon dried oregano
1 stalk celery	2 cloves wild garlic
2 potatoes, cubed	6 ripe tomatoes, quartered
2 large onions, cubed	1 tablespoon fresh basil
2 cups corn kernels	

Simmer the whole chicken, with water to cover, in a large covered kettle, with the bayberry leaves, parsley, and celery stalk, for 2 hours. When the meat seems tender, remove the chicken from the pot; cool slightly. Separate the meat from the bones and return the meat to the broth.

Add all remaining ingredients to the kettle, except the tomatoes and basil, and simmer for 30 minutes, or until the vegetables are tender. Add the tomatoes and basil and simmer for 10 minutes more. Serve at once, with corn dumplings (see recipe below) if desired.

CORN DUMPLINGS (serves 12)

2 cups fine cornmeal	1 cup nut milk (see page 7)
1 teaspoon crushed dried mint leaves	2 tablespoons nut oil (see page 7)

Blend all ingredients together into a soft dough. Drop the dumplings by spoonfuls into the steaming stew broth during the last 15 minutes of cooking time. Cover the pot and steam.

*Yeffe Kimball and Jean Anderson, *The Art of American Cooking* (Garden City, N.Y.: Doubleday & Co., Inc. 1965), pp. 166-167.

ROAST SADDLE OF VENISON
WITH WILD RICE (serves 12)

one 5-pound saddle of venison, dressed
    and severed for easy carving
dried juniper berries

peppercorns
6 to 8 strips thick-sliced bacon

Basting Marinade:

2 tablespoons honey or maple syrup
2 cups cider

Stud the saddle of venison with juniper berries and peppercorns. Lay the bacon strips over and secure with toothpicks. Stand the saddle on a rack in a large roasting pan.

Prepare the basting marinade by simmering the honey (or maple syrup) in the cider in a small saucepan until it is well dissolved and steaming.

Roast, basting often, for 1½ hours in a preheated 350° F oven. Cool the roast for 20 minutes. Carve, serving 1 rib per portion.

Serve on a bed of wild rice, together with the pan drippings.

STEWED WILD RABBIT
AND DUMPLINGS (serves 10)

one 5-pound wild rabbit, dressed and
    cut up for stewing
³/₄ cup corn oil
1½ cups fine cornmeal
2 quarts water
2 tablespoons wood ashes (see page 4)
    or ¼ cup cider vinegar

12 dried juniper berries
12 small onions
8 carrots
2 sprigs fresh dillweed

Rub each piece of rabbit with a little oil and lightly dust with the cornmeal. Brown each piece in hot oil, in a large kettle, turning until evenly seared. Add the water and ashes (or vinegar) and simmer, covered, for 1½ hours. Add the remaining ingredients and simmer for 30 minutes more. Serve hot.

Dumplings:

2 cups fine cornmeal

1 tablespoon wood ashes, optional (see page 4)

1 egg, beaten

1 tablespoon nut butter (see page 9)

1 cup water

Thoroughly blend all ingredients together. Drop the dumpling batter by spoonfuls into the simmering rabbit gravy. Cover and steam for 15 more minutes. Serve hot.

SPICEBUSH
Lindera benzoin

RACCOON PIE (serves 10 to 12)

1 large raccoon

4 cups water

2 cups vinegar

2 tablespoons coltsfoot ashes, optional (see page 27)

¹/₄ cup pickling spices

2 onions, diced

4 potatoes, chopped

4 carrots, chopped

2 green peppers, diced

1 tablespoon maple syrup

1 tablespoon dried spicebush berries

4 tablespoons cornstarch

biscuit dough

Raccoons and muskrats are dark-meat animals, and when properly prepared, they make excellent and tasty dishes. All layers of fat, inside and out, must be removed before cooking. The small round scent glands located under the armpits of the front legs and in the small of the back on either side of the spine must also be removed.

Cut the dressed raccoon into serving-sized pieces and place these in a mixture of the water, vinegar, coltsfoot ashes, and pickling spices for 8 hours, or overnight. Drain, reserving this brine, and place the meat in a large stewing kettle. Cover with fresh water and add 1 cup of the reserved brine. Cook for 1 ½ hours, or until tender. Then add the onions, potatoes, carrots, and peppers. Simmer until the vegetables are tender.

Remove the meat and the vegetables from the broth and place them in a large baking dish. Thicken the broth with cornstarch, and season to taste with the maple syrup and spicebush berries. Blend thoroughly, then pour this mixture over the meat and vegetables. Cover the top with your best biscuit dough. Slice a vent in the top. Bake the pie in a preheated 450° F oven until golden brown — about 20 minutes.

Muskrat pie and rabbit pie may be prepared in much the same way, varying the vegetables and the seasonings to taste.

PARTRIDGE OR ROAST DUCK STUFFED WITH APPLES AND GRAPES (serves 4 to 6)

2 partridge or one 5- to 6-pound duck,   2 cups cider for basting
   dressed

Stuffing:

giblets
½ pound fresh mushrooms, chopped
2 cups Concord or wild grapes, halved
   and seeded
6 to 8 whole potatoes, unpeeled
   (optional)

4 green apples, cored and chopped
2 cups shelled dried hazelnuts
1 tablespoon juniper berries
pinch of dillweed
6 medium whole onions (optional)
6 carrots, cut into thirds (optional)

Simmer the giblets in 2 cups water for 40 minutes. Lift out the giblets, cool slightly, then chop and return to the liquid in the pot. Add all the stuffing ingredients and mix together thoroughly.

Clean the fowl, removing any pin feathers and singeing to remove any hairs. Stuff the neck and body cavities; skewer and truss. Prick the skin well all over with a sharp fork to allow the excess fat to run off. Place the fowl on a rack in a large roasting pan, surrounding with the potatoes, onions, and carrots if desired.

Roast for 1 hour in a preheated 400° F oven, pricking the skin and basting it with the cider every 20 minutes. Reduce the oven temperature to 350° F and continue roasting for 2 hours more, pricking the skin and basting twice more.

TURKEY WITH OYSTER-CORNBREAD-RAISIN STUFFING* (serves 12)

one 12-pound turkey, dressed

Stuffing:

giblets

8 cups crumbled cornbread or
    johnnycakes
5 scallions, diced (including tops)
10 medium-sized fresh mushrooms,
    chopped
1 cup shelled dried black walnuts
1 cup raisins
1 cup sunflower seed butter (see page 8)
5 tablespoons oyster liquid for basting

2 tablespoons chopped fresh parsley
1/2 teaspoon chopped fresh savory
18 oysters, shucked and chopped (reserve
    liquid)
1 egg
1 clove garlic, crushed
5 tablespoons giblet broth
1/2 cup drippings
3 tablespoons cornmeal

Prepare the cleaned, dressed turkey for stuffing. In a covered saucepan, simmer the giblets in 1 1/2 cups water for 30 minutes. Remove, cool, and chop. Return to the cooled broth and save for gravy.

Thoroughly mix all the stuffing ingredients together in a large bowl. Lightly stuff the neck and body cavities of the turkey; do not pack. Skewer the openings together and truss the legs together.

Place the turkey, breast side up, in a large roasting pan. Rub the bird generously with 1/4 cup of the sunflower seed butter.

Roast the turkey, uncovered, in a preheated 325° F oven, basting every 30 minutes with a mixture of 5 tablespoons of the oyster liquid and the juices from the bird. Also dot every hour or so with spoonfuls of the remaining 3/4 cup sunflower seed butter. Roast for approximately 6 hours, allowing 40 minutes per pound as a guide. The bird is done when the legs move easily at the joint.

Giblet gravy should be made in a saucepan over medium heat, after the turkey is finished and being carved (but prior to serving). Add 1/2 cup of the seasoned drippings from the turkey to the giblets and broth. Bring to a boil, add the cornmeal, and simmer, stirring continually until the gravy thickens and is creamy. Serve hot.

*Courtesy of Ella Thomas/ Sekatau of the Narragansett peoples.

QUAIL WITH HAZELNUTS (serves 4)

4 quail, dressed
¹/₄ cup sunflower seed oil (see page 8)
1 cup fine cornmeal
¹/₄ cup nut butter (see page 9)
1 cup hot water

2 tablespoons wood ashes, optional (see page 4)
1 cup wild grapes, seeded
¹/₂ cup shelled hazelnuts, chopped

Rub the quail inside and out with the sunflower seed oil and roll in the cornmeal to coat the skins lightly. Melt the nut butter in a skillet and sauté the quail, turning often, over medium heat, until they are well browned. Add the water, ashes, and wild grapes, cover, and simmer over low heat for 45 minutes, stirring once or twice to blend.

Toast the hazelnuts in a shallow pan in a 350° F oven, until light brown — about 10 minutes. Serve each quail on a bed of rice or tender greens, and spoon over each bird the hot, toasted hazelnuts.

STUFFED ROAST GOOSE (serves 10 to 12)

one 10- to 12-pound goose, dressed
2 cups cider for basting

whole onions (optional)
apples (optional)

Stuffing:

goose giblets
¹/₄ pound fresh mushrooms, chopped
2 cups fine white cornmeal
1 tablespoon chopped fresh dillweed

2 cups dried currants or fresh cranberries, chopped
1 tablespoon honey
1 teaspoon chopped fresh spicebush leaves

Simmer the goose giblets in 1 quart water for 40 minutes. Lift out the giblets and cool slightly, then chop. Return the giblets to 1¹/₂ cups of the broth and combine with the rest of the stuffing ingredients. Mix thoroughly.

Clean the goose, remove the pin feathers, and singe off any hairs. Stuff the neck and body cavities. Skewer and truss. Place the goose, breast side up, on a rack in a large roasting pan. Surround with whole onions and apples if desired. Roast, uncovered, in a preheated 350° F oven for 4¹/₂ hours. Prick the skin well with a fork and baste with the cider and drippings every 30 minutes.

Gravy:

Reserve the drippings in the bottom of the roasting pan after removing the goose (to stand and cool before carving). Tip the pan and skim off the fat. Return the pan with the drippings to low heat. Add 2 tablespoons cornstarch to $1/2$ cup water, then add to the hot drippings, stirring until thick and bubbling. Keep hot and serve beside the goose, for use over the meat, vegetables, or wild rice.

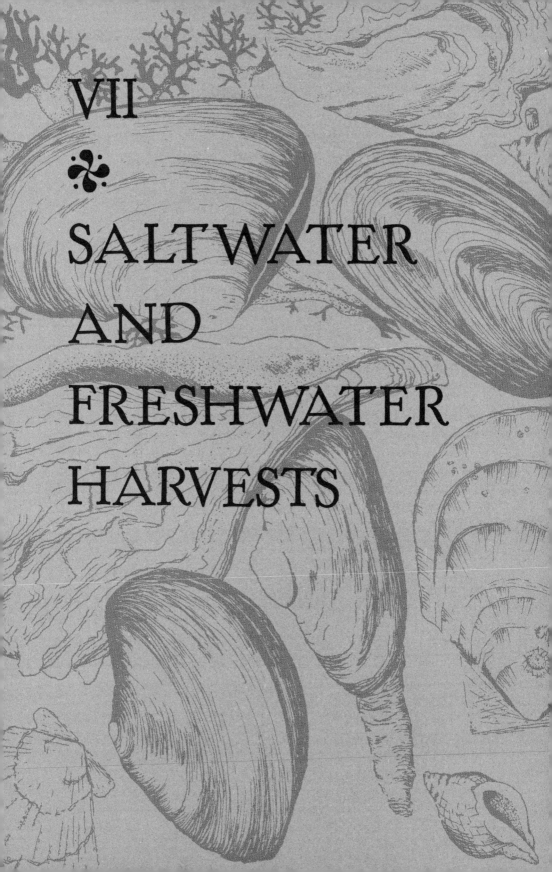

VII

❧

SALTWATER AND FRESHWATER HARVESTS

Seasonally many northeastern Indian tribes migrated to the bays and Atlantic coastal areas, seeking the abundance of foods from the sea and salt marshes. Accompanied by feasting and ceremonial celebrations, these periods offered a welcome change from the Indians' woodland diet. Many of the seafood classics we enjoy today evolved during these coastal migrations.

The earliest migration was for the April fishing season for shad, harbinger of spring, and foretold by the blossoming shadbush (shadblow).

SHAD is a variety of saltwater fish related to the herring but having a meatier body. They spawn in the rivers that come together along the North Atlantic coast. A valuable spring food to the Eastern Woodlands Indian tribes, shad is still considered a delicacy today.

Shad is very bony, each fish containing up to seven hundred bones in its body, and great care is necessary to clean and debone them into 4-inch fillets before preparing them for broiling, baking, or stewing.

BAKED SHAD WITH WILD LEEKS
AND NANNYBERRIES *(serves 6)*

1 medium shad, split and boned	1 cup nannyberries or raisins
2 tablespoons nut butter (see page 9)	½ cup cider vinegar
1 tablespoon chopped fresh parsley	garlic mustard sauce (see
1 cup wild leek bulbs	page 28)

Place the shad in a long greased baking dish. Mix the remaining ingredients (except the sauce) loosely together. Stuff the shad with half the mixture, sprinkle the rest over the outside, and bake in a preheated 375° F oven for 45 to 60 minutes. Baste once or twice with the juices.

Serve with herb rice and garlic mustard sauce.

BONELESS BAKED SHAD *(serves 8)*

one 3- or 4-pound shad	1 tablespoon sunflower seed butter (see
1 quart water	page 8)
¼ cup cider vinegar	ground dried spicebush berries to taste
3 tablespoons shelled sunflower seeds	1 cup chopped fresh sorrel leaves

Boil the shad in the water and vinegar in a large enamel kettle for 20 minutes. Drain, rinse, and place in a heavy roaster. Season with the sunflower seeds, sunflower seed butter, and spicebush berries and pour ¼ cup water around the fish. Cover tightly and bake in a preheated 250° F oven for 5 hours. By this method the smaller bones are completely dissolved, leaving the fish tender and delicious. Serve on a bed of fresh sorrel leaves.

PLANKED SHAD *(serves 8)*

Prepare initially as for Boneless Baked Shad (see recipe above), but after steaming for 5 hours, remove the head, tail, and fins. Slit along the backbone and open gently into two halves (skin side down) on a well-greased oak plank. Season to taste and broil for approximately 20 to 30 minutes. Serve with boiled groundnuts, chopped potatoes, or wild rice and chopped fresh drillweed. Serve hot on a bed of sorrel or garlic mustard leaves.

SHAD ROE AND MILT

Shad is principally sought in its spawning season for the creamy male sperm (known as milt or soft roe) and the female sac full of eggs (known as hard roe). Both may be marinated raw in the refrigerator 2 weeks in a blend of vinegar, onions, spices, and oil, or they may be parboiled for 3 to 12 minutes in slowly simmering water, then quickly fried in nut butter to a golden, delicate doneness. When preparing hard roe, the membrane surrounding the eggs must be pricked several times with a needle to prevent it from bursting and scattering the minute eggs.

HERRING OR MACKEREL
ROE AND MILT (serves 8)

A rich, delicious treat that must be delicately handled in preparation.

Save the sac of roe and milt from 2 fish; wash lightly then chill or freeze until preparation time.

Place the roe and milt, one at a time, in a medium pot of boiling water (with 1 teaspoon cider vinegar added) and simmer for 5 minutes. Remove and carefully drain, sauté quickly, on all sides, in nut butter, or broil in a greased baking dish for 15 minutes.

This delicacy is usually served as an appetizer and may be placed on a bed of fresh sorrel or violet leaves, and flanked with hard-boiled eggs and chopped fresh dillweed.

BLUEFISH is found, at various seasons, along the entire length of the Atlantic coast. Its name is derived from the bluish tinge of its skin and flesh. This dark-meated fish is rich and flavorful and may be prepared in a variety of ways.

SHEEP–SORREL
Rumex acetosella

BAKED BLUEFISH (serves 6)

1 large bluefish
1 teaspoon ground dried juniper berries
1 teaspoon coltsfoot ashes, optional (see page 27)
3 tablespoons shelled sunflower seeds
1 teaspoon celery seeds

1 tablespoon chopped fresh dillweed
1 tablespoon chopped onion
2 tablespoons nut oil (see page 7)
1 cup chopped fresh sorrel leaves
1/2 cup wild onions, coarsely chopped

Clean and split the bluefish. Place in a well-greased pan; season inside and out with a mixture of juniper berries, coltsfoot ashes, sunflower seeds, celery seeds, dill, and onion. Sprinkle generously with nut oil and bake in a preheated 375° F oven for 1 hour. Serve steaming hot on a bed of fresh sorrel leaves and wild onions.

Bluefish cheeks are considered a delicacy by most Amerindians.

BAKED STUFFED BLUEFISH (serves 6)

one 4-pound bluefish, split and cleaned
2 tablespoons oil
pepper
choice of herbs to taste (tarragon, cumin, sage, dillweed, etc.)
1 cup chopped fresh mushrooms
1 cup shucked oysters and liquor
1 cup shelled chestnuts, chopped

1 scallion, chopped (including top)
1 clove garlic, crushed
1 tablespoon maple syrup
2 cups cornmeal
1 cup cider
1/4 teaspoon ground dried sassafras (young leaves)

Wipe the clean fish inside and out with the oil. Season with pepper and choice of herbs.

Mix the remaining ingredients (except the cider and sassafras) into the cornmeal; blend thoroughly and stuff the fish cavity.

Lay the oiled, stuffed, and seasoned fish on a large aluminum foil sheet in a long roasting pan. Fold and wrap the foil tightly around the fish, allowing a vent slit for steam to escape. Bake for 1 hour in a pre-heated 350° F oven, basting several times through the vent hole with the cider. Sprinkle with sassafras at the very end, after removing from heat.

COD, which gave its name to New England's best-known cape, is one of the most valuable and versatile fish, abundant year-round in our coastal waters. A mainstay of the coastal Indians' diet, cod was also favored by the colonists. Fresh cod is best during late fall. The head and shoulders are usually gently boiled (wrapped in cheesecloth), and the remaining fish is sliced and fried or broiled.

Scrod is young cod, no more than two pounds in size, and is usually broiled.

BROILED SCROD (serves 4)

Clean and split the scrod, removing the head, tail, and backbone. Place the fish, flesh side up, in a greased pan. Sprinkle with sunflower seed oil (see page 8) and dillseed. Broil for about 20 minutes, or until golden. Serve hot with wild greens and cranberries.

CODFISH BALLS (serves 10)

3 pounds fresh cod or salmon or halibut
4 cups diced unpeeled potatoes
2 cups water
1/4 teaspoon ground pepper
2 tablespoons oil

2 teaspoons maple syrup
choice of herbs to taste (dillweed, parsley, marjoram, etc.)
4 cups oil or fat for deep frying

Boil the fish and potatoes in a covered pot for 25 minutes. Drain and mash. Add the remaining ingredients (except the oil for deep frying) and shape into 2-inch balls. Deep fry in hot oil (or fat), stirring until golden. Drain on brown paper and serve either hot or cold.

COD TONGUES AND CHEEKS

Boil these delicate morsels for just a few minutes and serve with your favorite sauce, or dip in nut milk, roll in cornmeal, and sauté. Serve either hot or cold on a nest of fresh wild leek greens.

PICKLED FISH (serves 12)

one 4-to 5-pound fish
2 medium onions, thinly sliced
3 cups cider vinegar
12 dried juniper berries, crushed
12 peppercorns

1 tablespoon chopped fresh dillweed or 1
   tablespoon dillseed
1 tablespoon wood ashes, optional (see
   page 4)

Mackerel, herring, cod, halibut, tuna, striped bass, swordfish, and others may be well preserved by pickling. Clean and section the fish into medium-sized segments and place these on a bed of thinly sliced onions in a crock or glass container. Simmer the cider vinegar with the juniper berries, peppercorns, and chopped fresh dillweed (or dillseed), for 10 minutes. Stir in the wood ashes. Pour this mixture over the fish and onions to cover (add more vinegar if necessary). Cover and let stand in a cool place or in the refrigerator for 2 days to 2 weeks before serving. After 2 days the vinegar and spices should have softened and almost dissolved all internal bones. Serve cold, complemented with a wild salad composed of seasonal favorites. (The lemony sourness of sorrel makes it a fine companion to most fish.)

CREAMED OYSTERS (serves 8)

1 cup sunflower seed butter (see
   page 8)
2 cups fine cornmeal
2 cups small shucked oysters

1/4 cup hickory milk (see page 7) or
   medium cream
1/2 tablespoon ground dried spicebush
   berries

Melt the seed butter in a saucepan. Add the cornmeal, stir, and blend until crumblike. Spread 1 cup of this mixture evenly across the bottom of a shallow baking dish. Add the oysters, evenly spaced on the bed of cornmeal. Sprinkle with the hickory milk or cream and season with the spicebush berries. Top with the remaining cornmeal crumbs. Bake for 20 minutes in a preheated 350° F oven. Serve hot.

SPICED OYSTERS (serves 8)

2 cups large shucked oysters and liquor
cider vinegar
1/2 tablespoon chopped onion

1/2 tablespoon ground dried spicebush berries
2 cups water

Scald the oysters in their own liquor briefly, until just plump. Strain and reserve the liquor; add an equal amount of cider vinegar. Mix this liquid with the onion and spicebush berries and add to the water in a saucepan. Simmer for 10 minutes, skim, and strain over the cooled oysters. Let stand in a cool location or refrigerate for 24 hours before serving.

BAKED CLAMS (OR OYSTERS) ON THE HALF SHELL

freshly opened clams or oysters on
    half shell
cornmeal
oil

ground pepper
chopped fresh parsley
chopped sea lettuce

Place the clams (or oysters) in their half shells in a baking dish. Sprinkle with a mixture of the remaining ingredients. Bake in a preheated 325° F oven for 20 minutes, or until golden. Serve hot.

OYSTER PATTIES (serves 4 to 6)

2 cups mashed potatoes or Jerusalem
    artichokes
2 eggs, beaten
1 small onion, minced
1 tablespoon coltsfoot ashes, optional
    (see page 27)
2 tablespoons nut milk (see page 7)

1 tablespoon chopped fresh parsley
1 teaspoon mustard seeds
dillseed to taste
12 dozen shucked oysters
garnish: additional chopped fresh parsley
    and sorrel leaves

Blend all ingredients (except the oysters) into the mashed potatoes (or Jerusalem artichokes) and form into little cakes. Gently split each cake with a small spoon and push 1 or 2 oysters into the center, then press the cake back into shape. Brush each cake with additional nut milk and sprinkle the moist tops with dillseed. Bake in a preheated 375° F oven until golden — about 30 minutes. Garnish with parsley and lemony-flavored sorrel leaves. Serve hot.

CLAMBAKE *(serves 6)*

2 dozen fresh oysters, in the shell, cleaned

six 1- to 1½-pound fresh (green) lobsters

6 ears corn, in the husk

6 medium potatoes, unpeeled

3 dozen fresh mussels, in the shell, cleaned

2 dozen fresh clams, in the shell, cleaned

2 quarts water

2 whole scallions

Place the oysters in the bottom of a very large, deep kettle. Add 3 of the lobsters, 3 of the ears of corn, the 6 potatoes, then the 3 remaining ears of corn and the 3 remaining lobsters. Place the mussels and clams in and around the other foods. Pour in the water, and place the scallions on top. Cover the kettle and bring to a boil. Lower heat and simmer for 1 hour, or until the potatoes are tender. Serve hot.

STEAMED CLAMS *(2 cups per person)*

Refrigerate freshly dug clams overnight in seawater to which ¼ cup cornmeal has been added. By morning the clams will have flushed most of the sand and grit out of their systems.

Place the clams in a heavy kettle, cover with water, and add a celery stalk and 1 teaspoon dillseed for flavor. Bring to a boil over medium heat, cover the kettle, and remove from heat. Steam off heat for 20 minutes. Serve hot with drawn butter or your favorite sauce.

CLAM CHOWDER *(serves 6 to 8)*

1 large onion, chopped

2 large cloves garlic, crushed

¼ pound butter

2 dozen clams, steamed, shucked, and diced

2 large unpeeled potatoes, diced

2 cups clam broth

2 cups light cream or milk, or 2 cups stewed tomatoes

2 cups diced celery

garnish: ground pepper and chopped chives to taste

Sauté the onion and garlic in the butter in a deep kettle until golden. Add the remaining ingredients and simmer slowly until the potatoes are tender—about 30 minutes. Serve hot, garnished with pepper and chives. Oysters or mussels may be substituted for the clams.

BROILED MUSSELS (serves 4)

4 dozen mussels, in the shell, scrubbed
    well
2 cups boiling water
2 cups mussel broth
1 clove garlic, chopped

1 cup fine cornmeal
1/4 cup chopped fresh parsley or sea
    lettuce
1/2 cup oil

Steam the mussels in the water for 10 minutes, until tender. Place the mussels on the half shell in a flat pan, pour the broth over them, and sprinkle with the garlic and cornmeal. Top with the parsley or sea lettuce. Sprinkle oil over all. Broil until lightly browned.

STEAMED MUSSELS OR MUSSEL SOUP (serves 4)

2 quarts mussels, in the shell, scrubbed
    well
1 quart boiling water
1/2 pound butter

1 cup chopped celery
1/2 cup chopped leeks (including tops)
1 cup cider vinegar

Place all ingredients in a heavy pot and cover with boiling water. Cover and steam until the mussels are fully opened — about 10 minutes. (Overcooking will make the mussels tough and less flavorful.)

Serve hot in bowls with its own buttered broth, seasoned with ground pepper and chopped fresh parsley.

STEAMED MUSSELS AND HALIBUT (serves 4)

2 dozen blue Atlantic mussels, in
    the shell
2 center slices of halibut (about 2
    pounds)
1 cup cider vinegar

1/4 cup chopped fresh parsley
1/4 cup oil
2 scallions, chopped (including tops)
1/2 teaspoon dillseed
pinch of ground pepper

Scrub the mussels well with a stiff brush. Line a shallow baking pan with a 2-foot-long strip of heavy-duty aluminum foil. Coat the center of foil lightly with oil. Place the 2 halibut steaks on the foil, surround and top with the mussels and a mixture of the vinegar, parsley, oil, scallions, dillseed, and pepper. Wrap and seal the package tightly to steam the enclosed ingredients. Bake in a preheated 350° F oven for 45 minutes.

Remove from oven, cool slightly. Open the package and serve portions over plates of wild rice or corn mush, with wild grapes, currants, or cranberries.

CONCH (WHELK) STEW (serves 6 to 8)

1 or 2 channeled or knobbed pear conches (whelks), in the shell, scrubbed well
3 quarts water
2 stalks celery, chopped coarsely

$\frac{1}{2}$ cup cider vinegar
2 ripe tomatoes, diced
pinch of ground pepper
pinch of dillseed
pinch of dried sage

Boil the conches in the water with the celery and vinegar for 30 minutes. Drain and reserve the broth. When cooled slightly, pull the meat out of the shells and slice off the long, muscular foot. Discard the remaining body. Cut the foot into thin slices and return the meat to the simmering broth. Add the tomatoes and herbs. Simmer and blend for 10 minutes more. Serve steaming.

QUAHOG FRITTERS (serves 8)

2 dozen quahogs, in the shell, cleaned
$2\frac{1}{2}$ cups boiling water
2 cups fine cornmeal
1 egg, beaten
1 teaspoon dillseed

1 tablespoon wood ashes, optional (see page 4)
1 tablespoon coltsfoot ashes, optional (see page 27)
$\frac{1}{4}$ cups corn oil for frying

Steam the quahogs in the water in a covered kettle until they open. Drain and reserve the broth. Remove the quahogs from their shells and chop. Place them in a bowl with 1 cup of the broth and add the remaining ingredients, blending thoroughly into a light batter. Drop by tablespoonfuls onto a hot greased griddle; fry quickly, flipping once, until golden.

Serve with wild greens and the remaining shellfish broth.

SCALLOPS are delicate, fluted shellfish native to North Atlantic waters. The large deep-sea scallop is readily available, while the smaller bay scallop is in shorter supply. In general, only the adductor muscle, which holds the mollusk's shells together, is eaten.

Most coastal Indian tribes enjoyed the whole shellfish, freshly opened and raw. Traditionally they ate all they could immediately; especially abundant catches were kept over a period of days by cooking and spicing, or smoking and drying.

FRIED SCALLOPS (serves 4)

2 pounds shucked bay or deep-sea
   scallops
1 egg, beaten

2 cups fine cornmeal seasoned to taste
   with ground dillseed and wood
   ashes (see page 4)
1/4 cup nut oil (see page 7)

Dip the clean, dry scallops into the egg, then roll in the seasoned cornmeal. Heat the oil and fry for about 2 to 5 minutes, or until golden. Serve on wild rice with chopped fresh sorrel leaves and parsley.

LONG ISLAND SCALLOP STEW (serves 6)

2 cups nut milk (see page 7) or
   medium cream
1 tablespoon coltsfoot ashes, optional
   (see page 27)

2 dozen bay scallops, shucked
2 tablespoons fine cornmeal

Combine all ingredients and simmer for 20 minutes. Serve on a platter of chopped fresh sorrel leaves and chopped dillweed.

SPICED RAW SCALLOPS (serves 4)

3 dozen bay scallops
2 tablespoons sunflower seed oil (see
   page 8)
1 clove garlic, chopped

1 small onion, diced
4 dried bayberry leaves
1 cup cider vinegar

Combine all ingredients, blend, and chill overnight. Serve over chopped fresh parsley, dillweed, and mint leaves.

SEA HARVESTS

KNOBBED PEAR CONCH

ROCK PURPLE

IRISH MOSS
Chondrus crispus
SURF CLAM
BLUE MUSSEL

QUAHOG

LONG-NECKED CLAM

SEA SCALLOP

EASTERN OYSTER

COMMON PERIWINKLE

BAY SCALLOP

SHRIMP AND SCALLOP PIE (serves 8 to 10)

80 raw shrimp
30 bay scallops
1 teaspoon chopped fresh parsley
1 cup water
2 cups fine cornmeal
4 ripe tomatoes, chopped

1 cup chopped celery
1 tablespoon nut oil (see page 7)
4 dried bayberry leaves, crumbled
3 cloves wild garlic, chopped
1 tablespoon dillseed

Combine all ingredients (except for the dillseed) and blend well. Place in a greased baking dish, sprinkle the top with the dillseed, and bake for 40 minutes in a preheated 350° F oven. Serve either hot or cold with herb rice and tomatoes sprinkled with parsley.

ROAST SEA SCALLOPS AND VEGETABLES (serves 8)

1 cup sunflower seed oil (see page 8)
1 tablespoon coltsfoot ashes, optional (see page 27)
1 teaspoon chopped fresh dillweed
2 dozen cherry tomatoes
1 dozen small green peppers, halved

2 dozen groundnuts or Jerusalem artichokes, scrubbed
2 dozen meadow mushrooms or chunks of giant puffballs
4 dozen sea scallops

Blend the sunflower seed oil, coltsfoot ashes, and dill; set aside. Alternate vegetable pieces with scallops on 8 skewers. Brush all the pieces with the seasoned oil; roast over a moderate fire for 15 to 20 minutes, turning and basting occasionally with what remains of the oil. Serve with fresh greens and wild rice.

SEAWEEDS are included among the algae. They are most prolific on rocky shores, where many are firmly anchored. Many species have air-filled bladders, so that when the tide comes in, the fronds float up toward the light. The many seaweeds have uses as food, medicines, and industrial ingredients. They are rich sources of minerals and vitamins.

DULSE *(Rhodymenia palmata)* is a sea alga found worldwide and has been a source of salt for centuries. Especially abundant in New England coastal waters (intertidal/subtidal zones), this flat, smooth red plant grows to about 1 inch long and washes onto beaches year-round. The rubbery dulse is easily dried, rolled, and stored for use as salty "fingers" to carry on hikes and camping trips as a mineral-rich chew.

EDIBLE KELP *(Alaria esculenta)* is olive-green to brown and 1 to 10 feet tall on short, cylindrical stems. It is found on submerged ledges and is washed ashore year-round. Brew it like a tea to render into a soup broth or chop it and add it to salads. All the kelps have an extremely high mineral content and make an excellent fertilizer.

IRISH MOSS *(Chondrus crispus)* is found all along the North Atlantic shore. It may be gathered all year round and dried and stored for use. The prepared jelly is a highly nutritious food, free of sugar and starch, high in sulphur and iodine, and excellent for restricted diets.

IRISH MOSS JELLY

Gather 1 cup Irish Moss and wash. Cover with 6 cups boiling water and boil for 30 minutes in a covered pot, stirring occasionally. Strain. Boil briefly in milk and flavor with wild fruits. Chill to serve.

LAVER *(Poryphyra vulgaris)* is a very thin, shiny ruffled frond about 1 foot long that washes ashore and may be harvested all year. It makes an excellent broth and a nutritious jelly; boiled until tender, it may be eaten as a vegetable. Or dry it and eat like dulse. A condiment may be created by cooking the fronds in water and lemon juice.

DULSE
Rhodymenia palmata

SEA LETTUCE. (*Ulva lactuca*) is a bright green, thin frond that is routinely washed up on shore. Use it dried and powdered as a saltlike seasoning or chop it and add it to salads. It is available all year round.

AMERICAN EELS are indigenous to the fresh and salt waters of the Atlantic and Gulf coasts of North America and are sought in both environments year-round. To the native Americans, eels were a highly prized, nutritious, and delectable food. Mature eels spawn in early spring, deep in the Sargasso Sea off Bermuda. During their early developmental stages they are widely dispersed by the coastal currents, but as they grow, they begin their migration into the estuaries along the coast. Eels are capable of crossing stretches of land in order to reach freshwater habitats, where they will remain (as elvers) for up to fifteen years. Finally maturing and undergoing a sexual metamorphosis, they begin their nocturnal migration back to the sea, to spawn in the depths of the Sargasso Sea.

SMOKED EEL STEW (serves 8)

one 1 1/2-pound smoked eel
4 potatoes, in their skins
4 yellow onions
1 tablespoon dried juniper berries
choice of herbs to taste

6 cups boiling water
garnish: ground pepper, chopped fresh
parsley, and grated cheese
(optional)

Clean and skin the eel; split and remove the backbone. Cut into 2-inch pieces. Simmer with the potatoes, onions, juniper berries, and herbs in the water in a large, heavy kettle for 1 hour. Skim off excess fat. Serve hot, topped with pepper, parsley, and grated cheese.

BAKED EELS (serves 10)

five 2-pound eels
3 cups groundnuts
3 cups wild leek bulbs
1/2 cup sunflower seed oil (see page 8)

1/2 cup cider or birch vinegar
1 tablespoon ground dried spicebush
berries
1 teaspoon chopped fresh dillweed

Clean, skin, and split the eels; remove the backbones and cut into 3-inch pieces. Surround the pieces in a large pan with the groundnuts and wild leek bulbs. Sprinkle with the remaining ingredients and bake in a preheated 350° F oven for 30 to 40 minutes.

QUICK-FRIED EELS *(serves 10)*

five 2- to 3-pound eels
2 cups fine cornmeal
1 teaspoon ground dried spicebush berries
1 teaspoon coltsfoot ashes, optional (see page 27)

1 teaspoon chopped fresh dillweed
½ cup sunflower seed oil (see page 8) or nut oil (see page 7)
garnish: chopped fresh dillweed or parsley

Clean, skin, and split the eels; remove the backbones and cut into 3-inch pieces. Drop them, 2 pieces at a time, into a "spice bag" containing a mixture of cornmeal, spicebush berries, coltsfoot ashes, and dill. Shake to coat each piece, then place the pieces in a hot cast-iron skillet containing sunflower seed (or nut) oil. Sear quickly on all sides to brown and seal in the juices.

Serve the fried eels on mounds of chopped ripe tomatoes, cooked squash, and rice. Garnish with dill or parsley. The meat can easily be eaten away from the tiny backbone vertebrae. It is tasty and juicy white meat.

Seasonally abundant freshwater fish and shellfish composed a significant share of the Eastern Woodlands Indians' diet. Prehistoric "midden heaps," or refuse deposits, yield the bones and shells of many species of freshwater fish, clams, and mussels.

TROUT, one of the salmon family, is perhaps the most delicate of all freshwater fish. The lake and brook trout are protein-rich and may be enjoyed in a variety of ways.

BAKED LAKE TROUT *(serves 2)*

one 3- to 4-pound lake trout
3 tablespoons sunflower seed oil (see page 8)

choice of herbs to taste (dillweed, parsley, basil, mint, etc.)
4 tablespoons fine cornmeal

Clean and split the trout; remove the head and backbone. Place in a greased baking pan, flesh side up, and sprinkle with the sunflower seed oil, herbs, and cornmeal. Bake in a preheated 350° F oven for 30 minutes.

TROUT CONSOMMÉ (serves 6)

8 cooked trout heads
5 cups boiling water

10 juniper berries
2 sprigs dillweed

Combine all ingredients in a pot and simmer for 30 minutes. Strain and serve hot, or chill and serve as an aspic garnished with hard-boiled eggs and herbs. This trout stock is also excellent to flavor vegetables.

CATFISH or BULLHEAD. A variety of fish (usually "whiskered") is grouped under this generic name, varying in size from one to a hundred pounds. If the fish is kept alive for twelve to twenty-four hours "after catch," until all the food in the stomach is digested, the flesh will be rich, sweet, and usually white.

FRIED CATFISH (BULLHEAD) (serves 10 to 12)

one 5- to 6-pound catfish
1 cup fine cornmeal

1 tablespoon chopped fresh dillweed
½ cup nut oil (see page 7)

Skin the fish before cooking; split; remove backbone. Roll the fish in the cornmeal seasoned with the dillweed, and fry in nut oil until golden. Serve with wild herbs and corn bread.

IROQUOIS SOUP — U'NEGA'GEI (serves 6)

two 3-pound fish (trout, bass, or haddock), cleaned but with the skin left on
3 quarts water
4 large fresh mushrooms, sliced
1 large yellow onion, diced
2 cups dried lima beans

2 tablespoons fine cornmeal
2 tablespoons chopped fresh parsley
1 clove garlic
½ teaspoon dried basil
garnish: fresh chopped dillweed and parsley

Place all ingredients in a large kettle and simmer, uncovered, for 30 minutes. Carefully lift out the fish, cool slightly; remove skin and bones. Flake the fish, then return it to the steaming pot (add pieces of fish skin if desired). Simmer for another 30 minutes, stirring frequently. Serve hot.

FISH BAKED IN CLAY

Pack any suitable fresh-caught fish (neither cleaned nor scaled) in a blanket of clay. Allow to dry for a few minutes by the fire; then bury this package in the hot coals, baking until the clay is hard (approximately 1 hour).

To serve, rake from the fire and hammer to break open the clay jacket. The cooked fish should split easily into 2 portions and the bones lift out. The intestines usually shrink into a tight ball and are easy to remove; the scales should be embedded in the clay. Sprinkle the steaming fish sections with your choice of herbs and nut oil (see page 7).

VIII

❖

NATURAL BREADS

Indians discovered the special properties of ashes mixed with foods or water. They saw that corn soaked in water with ashes became whiter and puffier and acquired a unique flavor. This became *hominy*, which was fermented into sour soup, fried with meats or wild greens, or baked into custardlike puddings. Hominy was also dried and pounded into grits, which became various other nutritious dishes.

HOMINY GRITS *(serves 8)*

5 cups water
1 cup hominy grits

1 tablespoon nut butter *(see page 9)*
1 tablespoon honey

Bring the water to a rapid boil in a saucepan. Gradually pour in the hominy grits, stirring; then add the nut butter and honey and stir. Cook for 20 minutes, or until all the water is absorbed.

Grits may be sweetened, if tastes dictate, or herb-seasoned instead. Hominy grits may be everything, from a steaming breakfast cereal to a lunch soup or side dish to a dinner vegetable.

FRIED HOMINY GRITS (serves 8)

1 recipe Hominy Grits, cooked and
   cooled (see page 118)

⅓ cup nut oil (see page 7)
   or bacon fat

Press the grits into 8 greased glasses; chill for at least 2 hours (preferably overnight). Unmold with the aid of a knife and slice into ½-inch-thick rounds. Heat the nut oil (or bacon fat) and brown for 8 minutes on each side. Serve hot as breakfast cakes. Great plain or topped with maple syrup.

Pones, "Hoecakes," or "Ashcakes" are flattened cakes of cornmeal and water. These everyday breads of southern tribes were usually baked directly in the campfire on stones or wooden paddles, or tossed into the glowing coals. By observing Indian cooks, the colonists learned to create the Indian breads, using Indian methods.

CORN PONE (serves 6)

1 cup cornmeal
½ cup nut milk (see page 7) or water

1 teaspoon baking powder
2 tablespoons bacon drippings

Mix the cornmeal, nut milk (or water), and baking powder together thoroughly. Grease a hot skillet with the bacon drippings. Drop the batter into the skillet by tablespoonfuls, shaping into 6 pone cakes. Brown for 10 minutes on each side. Serve hot.

Indian women were creative and experimental cooks. They sweetened their cornmeal batters with fresh or dried fruits and berries if available or with fragrant herbs, powdered roots, or small quantities of wood ashes.

GRUEL (serves 8)

3½ cups water
1¼ cups white cornmeal

1½ teaspoon maple syrup

Boil the water, then add the cornmeal and maple syrup, mixing well. Heat slowly, stirring frequently, for 10 minutes, or until smooth and thick. Serve in bowls, topped with maple sugar and cream if desired.

FRIED GRUEL (serves 8)

1 recipe Gruel, cooked and cooled   ¹/₄ cup oil for frying
    (see page 119)

Chill the gruel in 2 round tin cans or glasses for 2 hours. Unmold with
the aid of a knife and slice into rounds ¹/₂-inch thick. Heat the oil and
brown the slices well on both sides. Serve hot as bread or topped with
syrup as a breakfast dish.

CHIPPEWA BANNOCK (serves 6)

2 cups cornmeal   honey to taste or ¹/₂ cup berries
³/₄ cup water   ¹/₄ cup oil for frying
5 tablespoons fat or oil for seasoning

Blend the first three ingredients together and sweeten with the honey
(or berries). Heat the oil in a large skillet and drop tablespoonfuls of batter into it, flattening them into cakes. Cook 5 minutes per side, or until
golden. Enjoy either hot or cold. Good trail food.

INDIAN CAKE (BANNOCK) (serves 8)

1 cup white cornmeal   1 cup sour milk
¹/₂ cup cattail flour (see page 66)   1 egg, beaten
1 teaspoon wood ashes (see page 4) or   2 tablespoons honey
    baking soda   3 tablespoons corn oil
¹/₂ teaspoon ground ginger

Mix together the cornmeal and cattail flour in a large bowl. Gradually
add the remaining ingredients, blending well and working into a sturdy
dough. Turn into a well-greased loaf pan (8″ x 4″) and bake in a preheated 425° F oven for 30 minutes.

The dough may also be shaped and flattened into a greased cast-
iron skillet and cooked over an open fire, turning once. Gauge the
cooking time according to the fire, usually 10 minutes per side. Delicious as a dinner or trail bread, it is enhanced by the addition of a handful
or two of seasonal (or dried) berries included in the raw batter before
baking.

NAVAJO FRY BREAD (three 8-inch round breads)

2 cups flour

1 teaspoon coltsfoot ashes, optional (see page 27)

¹/₂ cup ground sunflower seeds

2 teaspoons baking powder

2 tablespoons oil

Work the first four ingredients into a dough ball, kneading until the texture is smooth. Place in a covered bowl or crock for 2 hours.

Remove the dough and cut it into 3 portions. Roll them into circle shapes, about 8 inches round and ¹/₂-inch thick. Cut 2 large, deep parallel slits across the tops.

Heat the oil in a heavy skillet and fry for 2 minutes on each side.

ELDERBERRY
Sambucus canadensis

ELDER BLOSSOM FRITTERS (serves 8)

2 cups fine white cornmeal

1 egg, beaten lightly

1 cup water

1 tablespoon maple syrup

¹/₄ cup corn oil for frying

16 elder blossom clusters, washed and dried

Prepare a light batter beating together the cornmeal, egg, water, and maple syrup. Heat the oil on a griddle and drop the batter by large tablespoonfuls onto it, immediately placing 1 blossom cluster in the center of each raw fritter and pressing lightly into the batter. Fry for 3 to 5 minutes, or until golden. Flip and fry for 3 minutes on the other side. Drain on brown paper. Serve hot, sprinkled with additional loose blossoms and maple sugar.

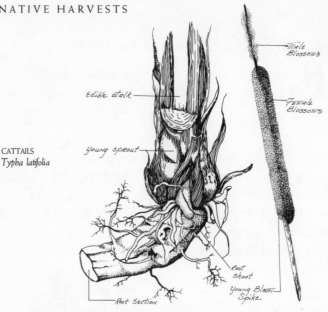

CATTAILS
Typha latifolia

Male Blossoms
Female Blossoms
Edible stalk
Young sprout
Root shoot
Young Bloom Spike
Root Section

Cattail Flour. During June the male blossoms, which are located above the female cattail bloom spike, produce quantities of bright yellow pollen. This nutritious, corn-flavored food substance is easily gathered by wading through cattail marshes and gently bending each bloom spike over a deep bowl or bucket and "dusting" the golden pollen in (thereby pollinating the plant at the same time). This gathering is best accomplished on a still, dry afternoon. Gather as much fresh pollen as you can use soon or put by. It is an important flour extender and makes a good addition to biscuit, bread, and cake batters. It should be added in an amount to replace an equal amount of flour deleted from a recipe.

CATTAIL POLLEN CAKES (serves 4)

1 cup sifted cattail pollen
1 cup fine white cornmeal or cattail
   flour (see page 66)
3 teaspoons finely chopped dried
   spicebush leaves

1 tablespoon honey
2 eggs, beaten lightly
1 1/2 cups water or broth
2 tablespoons sunflower seed oil (see
   page 8)

Thoroughly blend all ingredients together into a smooth batter. On a very hot greased griddle, ladle the batter out into 4 large cakes. Cook for 3 to 5 minutes, until bubbles form on the surface, then flip and finish cooking. Serve hot with nut butter (see page 9) and maple syrup.

HAZELNUT CAKES (12 to 14 small cakes)

½ pound shelled dried hazelnuts,
    unblanched and ground finely or
    pureed
2 cups water

1 teaspoon maple syrup
⅓ cup fine cornmeal
⅓ cup oil for frying

Boil the nuts in the water for 30 minutes, or until mushy. Add the maple syrup and cornmeal, stir well, and let stand for 20 minutes, or until thick.

Heat the oil in a skillet and drop the nut mixture by tablespoonfuls into the hot oil; brown on one side, flip, flatten into cakes, and brown on the other side. Drain on brown paper. Serve either hot or cold as a bread or breakfast treat.

PUMPKIN-HICKORY CAKES (yields 10 to 12 muffins)

2 cups fine cornmeal
1 cup potato flour (see page 66)
1½ cups stewed pumpkin meat, beaten
    smooth

¾ cup shelled dried hickory nuts,
    chopped
1 egg, beaten with 1 teaspoon water
½ cup maple syrup

Mix together the cornmeal and potato flour in a large bowl. Gradually add the remaining ingredients to the flours, blending thoroughly into a smooth batter. Pour into a well-greased loaf pan (9" x 5") and bake in a preheated 350° F oven for 1¼ hours, or until a toothpick inserted into the center of the loaf comes out clean. Or spoon the batter into greased muffin tins and bake until golden on top — about 25 minutes.

JOHNNYCAKE "NOKEHICK"* (yields 16 to 20 johnnycakes)

2 cups johnnycake white stone-ground
    cornmeal
4 tablespoons maple syrup
2 cups boiling water or 2 cups clam
    (quahog) juice

2 cups light or medium cream
¼ cup corn oil for frying

*Courtesy of Ella Thomas/Sekatau of the Narragansett peoples.

Add the cornmeal and maple syrup to the boiling water (or clam juice), stirring well. Boil for at least 20 minutes, or until thickened. Cool slightly, then thin the batter with the cream until it is firm, not runny. Drop by tablespoonfuls onto a medium-hot, well-greased griddle. Flip after 6 minutes and cook for another 5 minutes.

Johnnycakes were eaten as a cracker and enjoyed with soups and stews. They were also crumbled and used to stuff game, poultry, and squash.

INDIAN CORNMEAL DESSERT* (serves 10)

1 cup johnnycake white stone-ground
   cornmeal
2 cups cold water
¹/₄ cup nut butter (see page 9)
1 cup blackberry, blueberry, or
   raspberry juice

2 cups berries
1 teaspoon nutmeg
³/₄ cup cream
³/₄ cup maple syrup
3 eggs, beaten lightly

Soak the cornmeal in the water. Melt the nut butter in a large pot, add the cornmeal mixture, and slowly heat, stirring constantly, for 15 minutes, or until thickened. Add the berry juice, berries, and nutmeg and bring to a boil, stirring constantly. Add the cream and maple syrup, blending thoroughly. Add the eggs and remove from heat, stirring until the mixture stops bubbling. Serve either hot or chilled.

WILD STRAWBERRIES (*Fragaria vesca* and spp.) of June and July were considered a very special fruit by the Native Americans. Indian tribes celebrated this harvesting time with ceremonies and festivals.

These small, fragrant, wild fruits of the meadows and open woods were added to numerous dishes and pressed and dried for winter use.

*Courtesy of Ella Thomas/Sekatau of the Narragansett peoples.

WILD STRAWBERRY BREAD (serves 4 to 6)

1 cup fine cornmeal
1 cup flour
1 cup nut milk (see page 7) or water
2 tablespoons nut oil (see page 7)

1 egg, beaten
1/2 cup finely cut fresh strawberry leaves
1 teaspoon coltsfoot ashes (see page 27)
1 cup freshly picked wild strawberries

Combine the cornmeal and flour in a large bowl. In a separate bowl, mix together the nut milk (or water), nut oil, egg, strawberry leaves, and coltsfoot ashes. Add to cornmeal and flour mixture and blend well. Fold in the wild strawberries and turn the batter into a well-greased loaf pan (4" x 8"). Bake in a preheated 425° F oven for 40 minutes.

WILD STRAWBERRY
Fragaria vesca

IX

❖

WILDERNESS
BEVERAGES

Nature perennially provides a superabundance of flavorful botanicals for beverages that are healthful and rejuvenating, as well as refreshing. Natural beverages range from wild teas and tisanes to coffees, flavorings, and fruit drinks.

Indians depended largely on edible wild plants for their beverages. When the first settlers arrived, and for centuries afterwards as they were pushing their way westward, they followed suit. If these wild drinks had not been rich in Vitamin C, a vitamin which the body cannot store and which is necessary for the prevention and cure of scurvy, many pioneers could not have lived to open our frontiers.

At the time of the American Revolution, even in the communities where stores were well-stocked, many chose wild drinks rather than continue to use oriental tea, tinged with an English tax. When the Civil War tore the country apart, many northerners and southerners alike had to turn again to the wilds for their teas and coffees.*

Most early peoples instinctively used seasonally available wild botanicals to flavor drinking water, which was the most essential beverage of all. Many plants used in this way were somewhat tart or bitter, but bitterness was considered beneficial, a cleansing, strengthening tonic for the system. Natural saps from various trees and vines provided flavored sweetenings; and among many cultures sap alone was a delightful drink.

*Bradford Angier, *Feasting Free on Wild Edibles* (Harrisburg, Pa.: Stackpole Books, 1966), p. 161.

A growing knowledge of preferred beverage materials led to intriguing mixtures: blended herbal teas, tonics, fruit drinks, medicines, as well as the vinegars, beers, and wines. The fermentation process was known and practiced by most preliterate peoples, and numerous beverages were derived through fermentation, although the inherent alcoholic content was usually very low. Most drinks were imbibed for their specific beneficial effects, much as the medicines similarly used. Often only a fine line separated the two categories in native usage.

Some of the most common North American beverage botanicals are highlighted here, reflecting historical Indian and colonial usage. Many of these beverages can be enjoyed either hot or cold, and in abundance; others are better used in small amounts. In general, any beverage that requires a long steeping period may be reheated, provided it isn't boiled.

ACORN *(Quercus,* about sixty species). Acorn shells are roasted until they lose their astringent quality, then steeped in boiling water or sap for use as a wholesome coffee drink. Allowing 1 teaspoonful per cup, put the "coffee" in a saucepan and simmer for 15 minutes; strain and serve.

BARBERRY *(Berberis canadensis).* The American or Allegheny Barberry is a low, thorny shrub with yellow wood and inner bark. It has edible yellow six-petaled flowers yielding edible scarlet single-seeded berries, which are high in pectin. The young leaves are delicious raw as a trail snack or steeped in boiling water as a light tea (use 1 teaspoonful per cup and steep, covered, for 15 minutes). A nutritious acid "lemonade" is created by diluting the cooked berry juice, then sweetening it with honey or maple sap to taste.

BEARBERRY, Kinnikinnick, Mealberry, Upland Cranberry *(Arctostaphylos uva-ursi).* The dried leaves provide an astringent winter tea with a pleasantly bitter taste. Use 1 teaspoon per cup and steep, covered, for 15 minutes. This tea is considered soothing to the stomach.

BEECHNUT *(Fagus grandifolia).* Roast the husked beechnuts by an open fire (or in a preheated 300° F oven for 30 minutes) to crack the shells. Cool and shell the nuts, then dry further in moderate heat until they are brittle. Grind them fine with a rolling pin and place the "coffee" in a sealed jar until ready to use. To prepare: Allowing 1 teaspoonful per cut, put the "coffee" in a saucepan, cover with boiling water, and simmer for 15 minutes. Strain and serve.

BERGAMOT (*Monarda didyma*) is the red-blossoming Bee Balm or Oswego Tea, and WILD BERGAMOT (*M. fistulosa*) is its lilac- or pink-blossoming relative, along with six additional indigenous species of the mint family. The leaves, stems, and blossoms of these choice, vigorous herbs may be used in a natural tea, soothing for sore throats and settling for the stomach. Cover an entire stalk, minus the roots, in 2 quarts of boiling water; cover the pot and steep for 15 minutes. For an individual cup of tea, use 3 leaves and follow the same pro-
cedure. These herbs are a boost for
ordinary teas and contain the
antiseptic thymol.

BERGAMOT
Monarda didyma

BIRCH (*Betula*, over 14 spp.) is an important genus of deciduous trees tapped in early spring for their flavorful sap. Many tribes harvested this sap as a fresh, nutritious beverage. It was (and still is) used for birch beer and vinegars. By the end of "tapping season" the sap was the base for various teas, and botanicals were steeped in it for additional flavor and sweetness.

BLACKBERRY (*Rubus* spp.). The leaves make an excellent tea that relieves diarrhea. Steep several fresh leaves for 5 minutes in boiling water in a covered pot for a light, mild tea. Blackberry leaves were also an important ingredient in herbal tea mixtures. The fruits make an excellent juice for drinks. Raspberries, which come from the same family, may be used in the same way.

BLACK BIRCH, Cherry Birch, Sweet Birch (*Betula lenta*). The twigs and bark are a primary source of oil of wintergreen. A pleasing, golden woodland tea is derived by steeping fresh (or dried) bark chips and twigs in enough boiling water to cover for 15 minutes in a covered pot or cup.

BLUE COHOSH, Papoose Root, Squaw Root (*Caulophyllum thalictroides*). The bluish seeds are roasted, ground, and boiled to make an excellent coffee drink. Allowing 1 teaspoonful per cup, put the "coffee" in a saucepan and simmer for 15 minutes; strain and serve.

BORAGE (*Borago officinalis*). The leaves and blue blossoms are steeped in boiling water to make a soothing, healthful tea that is high in calcium and potassium. Muddle 2 to 3 fresh or dried leaves in the bottom of a cup; cover with boiling water and steep, covered, for 15 minutes. The same herbal parts may be steeped in wine to render a fine tonic.

CHICORY (*Cichorium intybus*). The leaves and blue blossoms are steeped to make a mild herbal tea that is a digestive aid, as well as a good "medicinal" to relieve mucus congestion. The roasted and ground root is brewed to make a caffeine-free coffee. Measure and brew like conventional coffee.

CLOVER (*Trifolium* spp.) and SWEET CLOVER (*Melilotus* spp.) have perennially provided fine teas. The leaves and blossoms of most species are choice food, tobacco, and tea materials. Steep $1/3$ cup fresh (or $1 1/2$ teaspoons dried) blossoms for 5 minutes in $1 1/2$ cups boiling water; add honey to taste.

COLTSFOOT (*Tussilago farfara*) and SWEET COLTSFOOT (*Petasites palmata* and spp.) contribute their flowers and leaves to medicines, seasonings, tobaccos, and teas. An excellent herb (or medicinal) tea is prepared by steeping 2 teaspoons flowers and/or leaves in $1 1/2$ cups boiling water in a covered pot for 30 minutes. Strain and sweeten with honey. This flavorful tea was enjoyed often, especially to ease coughs, colds, bronchial asthma, and diarrhea.

COMFREY (*Symphytum officinale* and spp.). This coarse, introduced perennial herb has been used for centuries. The leaves and roots were brewed (or stewed) in boiling water (or mulled wine) to make a soothing tea. Both fresh and dried materials were used, internally and externally. This plant is still considered one of the finest healing herbs. Comfrey's huge hairy leaves provide the base for many mixed teas, lending a sturdy bouquet and flavor. One leaf is enough for an entire pot of tea; steep, covered, for 5 to 15 minutes, depending upon the strength desired.

DANDELION *(Taraxacum officinale)*. This persistent, cosmopolitan herb (introduced from Europe to North America long ago) affords us many uses, reflecting centuries of both pioneer and Indian ingenuity. The blossoms are excellent for teas and wines; the roots (preferably second year or older) provide a delicious caffeine-free coffee. Dig, wash, and dry the lengthy taproot; slowly roast by a low fire or in a slow oven for several hours, until crisp and brown. Grind fine and store in an airtight container; this may be measured and brewed like conventional coffee.

DANDELION BUD
Taraxacum officinale

DEWBERRY *(Rubus* spp.) is a large group of perennial vines of the rose family. The black, shiny berries were used for fruit drinks and wines in late summer, but the prickly leaves were sought all season for tea. Muddle 3 to 5 leaves in the bottom of a cup, cover with boiling water, cover the cup, and steep for 5 minutes.

DILL *(Anethum graveolens)* is a strong-smelling introduced herb that escaped cultivation. Dill tea is made with water or white wine. Muddle 2 to 5 seeds in the bottom of a cup, cover with boiling water (or warmed wine), cover the cup, and steep for 15 minutes. Enjoy 1 to 2 cupfuls a day as a digestive aid and to stimulate the appetite.

DITTANY *(Cunila origanoides.)* This native perennial was utilized for hot beverages by numerous Indian tribes. A hot infusion of dittany leaves was drunk to ease cold symptoms. Add 1 tablespoon leaves to 1½ cups boiling water; steep, covered, for 15 minutes.

ELDERBERRY *(Sambucus canadensis)*. An indigenous shrub that had many native uses, elder flowers are excellent dried and steeped as a tisane (use 1 teaspoonful per cup and steep, covered, for 5 to 15 minutes) or added to other teas. Elder rob is a thick, sweetened syrup boiled down from the ripe purple-black berries. This was used as an elixir or was diluted with water to make a delicious fruit drink.

GOLDENROD *(Solidago* spp.*)* These hardy annuals/perennials were fa-vored by many tribes for both utility and beauty. Collect the fragrant leaves and flowers on a dry day and air-dry. Add 2 teaspoons dried leaves and flowers to a small pot of boiling water, cover, and simmer for 15 minutes; strain and sweeten with honey or maple sap. This is a light, smooth tea.

GRAPE *(Vitis* spp.*)*. Since prerecorded history the ripened grapes from numerous native wild vines have provided excellent beverages, from light teas to wines and vinegars. For a pleasant tea, crush a few grapes in the bottom of a cup and cover with boiling water; steep, covered, for 5 to 10 minutes.

Perhaps the grapevine's true virtue is its clear, watery sap, easily ob-tained by cutting or severing a sturdy portion of vine. This has saved lives in periods of drought, because the grapevine is capable of storing considerable amounts of liquid.

GROUND IVY
Nepeta hederacea

GROUND IVY, Gill-over-the-ground, Fieldbalm, Cat's-foot *(Nepeta heder-acea)*. Introduced from Eurasia, it is a perennial found in lawns, orchards, and gardens, in damp, rich, semishaded soil; it is widespread through-out the northern United States and southern Canada and April through June. The leaves and blossoms may be dried to make an en-joyable herb tea. Cover 1 teaspoon dried leaves with 1 cup boiling water; steep, covered, for 5 to 15 minutes.

ICELAND MOSS *(Cetraria islandica)*. This pale, skeletal lichen is excellent tea material. Boil 1 teaspoon of the dried plant in 1 cup water, covered, for 30 minutes. Strain, sweeten, and cool. This is a smooth, palatable tea, hot or cold. It may be mixed with nut milk (see page 7) or fruit juice for a pleasing variation.

JUNIPER. (*Juniperus communis* and spp.). Juniper berries (among many other uses) may be roasted and ground to become a coffee drink or added to other coffee mixtures. Measure and brew like conventional coffee. For a large gathering of people, juniper tea may be prepared by combining 20 fresh sprigs juniper, $\frac{1}{2}$ cup blue juniper berries, 2 quarts water, and 2 tablespoons honey in a kettle or pot. Bring to a boil, cover, lower heat, and simmer for 10 minutes. Strain and serve. This pale, fragrant beverage is quite high in vitamin C.

LABRADOR TEA (*Ledum groenlandicum*) is a low, boreal, evergreen shrub, the woolly leaves of which make fine tea leaves. Dry the leaves, then muddle 2 to 3 leaves in a cup and steep, covered with boiling water, for 10 minutes. Sweeten to taste.

LIFE EVERLASTING (*Gnaphalium polycephalum*). A favored native Indian herb, the whole blossoming plant may be dried for use as a very palatable, mild tea. Use 2 quarts boiling water and steep, covered, for 15 minutes.

LINDEN or Basswood (*Tilia americana* and spp.). These large, useful deciduous trees have long been associated with many Indian cultures. The bark and inner fibers have many technological uses. The fragrant, cream-colored blossoms and inner bark are also excellent tea materials. Steep 1 teaspoon fresh (or dried) blossoms in 1 $\frac{1}{2}$ cups boiling water in a covered pot for 10 minutes. Sweeten to taste. Excellent for colds.

LOVAGE (*Ligustrum canadense*) and SCOTCH LOVAGE (*L. scoticum*). These smooth perennial herbs provide excellent food and tea resources. Both the celerylike foliage and the large aromatic roots may be enjoyed fresh or dried (in moderate amounts). Add a small handful of leaves and roots to a quart of boiling water; steep, covered, for 15 minutes. Sweetening is hardly necessary. This pale, fragrant tea is mineral-rich and is a digestive aid.

MAPLE (*Acer* spp.). These trees were traditionally tapped by the Eastern Woodlands Indians in late winter and early spring for their clear, sweet sap, which is a bracing, nutritious drink. To refine its sweetness, the sap was simmered for hours until it yielded its amber syrup and sugar. This, in turn, was used to flavor many other beverages and foods. Extensively used as a seasoning prior to salt.

MINT (*Mentha* spp.) is fragrant perennial herbs, both wild indigenous and introduced varieties. Mint leaves are steeped fresh or dried in boiling water to render fine, light teas. Cover 1 tablespoon fresh leaves or 1 teaspoon dried with a cup of boiling water; steep, covered, for 5 to 15 minutes. Mint also enhances and boosts many other herbal and wild teas.

NEW JERSEY TEA (*Ceanothus americanus*) is a common indigenous herbaceous shrub of dry, gravelly soil. The leaves are highly prized for teas; steep 1 tablespoon fresh or 1 teaspoon dried in a cup of boiling water for 15 minutes and sweeten to taste. The dried root bark steeped in water was a fine sedative tea used by many eastern tribes. Some tribes used an infusion made of the whole plant to treat external skin disorders.

PENNYROYAL,   Squawbalm, Squawmint, Pudding-grass (*Hedeoma pulegioides*). This species was used frequently by numerous Indian tribes as a soothing tea to relieve headaches and cramps. Use 1 tablespoon fresh leaves and stems to 1 cup boiling water; steep, covered, for 15 minutes. Drink in moderation. A strong tea of this whole plant makes a good external skin wash for rashes and itching.

PENNYROYAL
Hedeoma pulegioides

PERSIMMON (*Diospyros virginiana*). The leaves are dried and steeped in boiling water, 1 teaspoonful per cup, for 10 minutes to create a light tea, very similar in flavor to sassafras. The ripe fruits, after the first frost, are mixed with other fruits in drinks and flavorings.

RASPBERRY (*Rubus* spp.). See Blackberry.

ROSE (*Rosa* spp.). A large family of native and introduced varieties, the ripe hips are prized for teas. The hips are very high in vitamin C, and the whitish seeds are high in vitamin E (grind to extract). For rose hip tea, steep 2 teaspoons crushed whole rose hips (either fresh or dried) in 1 quart boiling water in a covered pot for 10 minutes.

SASSAFRAS (*Sassafras albidum*). This deciduous tree was considered a panacea by both Indians and colonists. The leaves, roots, and bark were favored tea essentials. Muddle 2 or 3 fresh young leaves in the bottom of a cup, cover with boiling water, and steep, covered, for 10 minutes; or cover 1 tablespoon dried roots and bark with 2 cups boiling water and steep, covered, for 30 minutes. Indians used the pale red root infusion to reduce fevers and as a "spring tonic." Sassafras roots are believed to be the first plant product exported from New England. The first shiploads sailed from Cape Cod.

SPICEBUSH
Lindera benzoin

SPICEBUSH, Wild Allspice, Feverbush (*Lindera benzoin*). For centuries this noted member of the laurel family has provided an agreeable beverage. A pleasing tea is brewed from the aromatic leaves, twigs, and bark. Cover 3 to 5 fresh leaves with 1 cup boiling water and steep, covered, for 10 minutes; or cover 1 tablespoon dried roots and bark with 2 cups boiling water and steep, covered, for 30 minutes.

STRAWBERRY (*Fragaria* spp.) was sought for its green leaves and delicious fruits. Use it as you would blackberry.

STAGHORN SUMAC
Rhus typhina

SUMAC *(Rhus glabra* and *R. typhina)*. Sought for its ripe red berry clusters in late summer and fall through winter, pink sumacade (Indian "lemonade") is made by bruising 1 cupful of the red berries and then soaking them for 15 minutes in 1 quart hot (not boiling) water; cool and strain. This pleasing beverage is high in vitamins and in malic acid, which gives it the light citrusy taste. It does not require sweetening.

SUNFLOWER *(Helianthus* spp.). The hulls and seeds were roasted and ground, then brewed into a coffeelike drink by various Woodlands tribes. Measure and brew like conventional coffee.

SWEET FERN or MEADOW FERN *(Comptonia peregrina)*. The highly aromatic dark green leaves of this indigenous deciduous shrub were brewed into a warming tea by many Woodlands peoples. Cover one 10-inch branch with 2 quarts boiling water and steep, covered, for 20 minutes. This tea is so mild and light it does not require sweetening.

SWEET VERNAL GRASS *(Anthoxanthum odoratum)* is a perennial found in dry fields and meadows, and is widespread throughout the eastern and north-central states. It is best harvested in the spring and used as a fragrant herbal tea base. Use 1 teaspoon dried grass to 1 cup boiling water; steep, covered, for 10 minutes.

WILD CHAMOMILE (*Matricaria chamomilla*) and PINEAPPLE-WEED (*Matricaria matricarioides*) are low-growing, lacy perennials. Their small greenish-yellow flowerheads are daisylike, with tiny white rays. The foliage and blossoms have the fragrance of pineapple when disturbed or crushed. The fresh or dried blossoms are steeped to make an excellent pale golden, pineapple-scented tea. Use 1 teaspoonful per cup and steep, covered, for 5 minutes. This delicate beverage is calming and settling to the system, especially good to relieve flatulence or upset stomach. An infusion is also beneficial as a shampoo and hair rinse (especially for blonds). A strong, warm infusion is soothing for external ear treatments and can relieve earache. Finally, the same tea is a soil sweetener and will benefit the root systems of potted plants, particularly young seedlings.

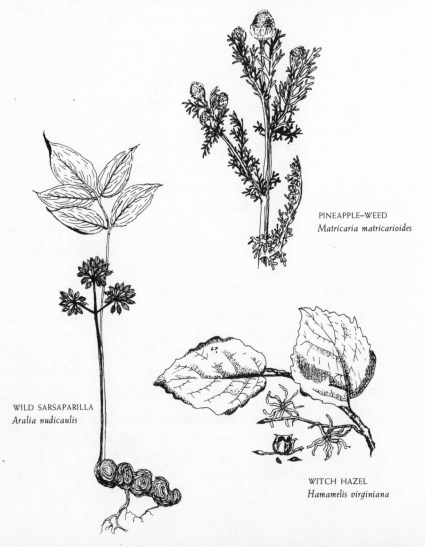

PINEAPPLE–WEED
Matricaria matricarioides

WILD SARSAPARILLA
Aralia nudicaulis

WITCH HAZEL
Hamamelis virginiana

WILD SARSAPARILLA (*Aralia nudicaulis* and spp.). This common woodland herb was sought for its aromatic roots, used to flavor beverages and medicines. A tea of the dried root was considered good for colds and rheumatism and was also used as a soothing external skin treatment. Steep 1 teaspoon dried, ground roots in 1 cup boiling water for 30 minutes.

WITCH HAZEL (*Hamamelis virginiana*). Sought for its beneficial properties by many Indian tribes, witch hazel was used as a tea primarily by the Iroquois and Cayuga peoples. This fine, refreshing woodland tea has a warming, nutlike flavor. Steep 5 fresh leaves (or 2 teaspoons dried leaves) in 2 cups boiling water in a covered pot for 5 minutes.

X

WILD
MEDICINES
AND
COSMETICS

The Indians, our first scientists, discovered in the plant world the sources and the secrets of healing. Aboriginal knowledge and usage of native botanicals were remarkable, unique, and accurate. The Indians had an exceptional understanding of laxative, diuretic, emetic, birth-control, and fever-reducing drugs. Foxglove (*Digitalis purpurea*) was correctly used by the Indians for its cardiac-stimulant properties for centuries before William Withering discovered digitalis in England in 1785.

Primitive Indian diets, often frugal, were generally better balanced than those of the early settlers, and the Indians were afflicted less frequently with vitamin-deficiency diseases.

During the bitter-cold winter of 1535–1536, the three ships of Jacques Cartier were icebound in the St. Lawrence River near the present site of Montreal. Isolated and starving, the company of 110 men barely subsisted until mid-March, by which time scurvy had become so rampant that 25 men had died and the rest were so weakened that there was little hope for their recovery. Cartier's auspicious encounter with the Laurentian Iroquois chief Domagaia (who had cured himself of the same disease earlier that winter) brought the Iroquois people to the aid of the dying crew. Iroquois women gathered branches of local hemlock and black spruce trees, boiled the bark and needles, and fed the Frenchmen the decoction. Those treated internally and externally readily recovered their health.

Although these Indians were unaware of vitamin C, their curative knowledge and skills had provided an effective remedy for scurvy, which most Europeans believed was caused by "bad aire." Reading of this incident more than two hundred years after Cartier's experience,

HEMLOCK
Tsuga canadensis

James Lind, a British naval surgeon, launched the experiments that proved the dietary-deficiency basis of scurvy. Indian medicine accomplished much of the "pharmaceutical spadework" to broaden new frontiers in medical history. Continuing research into Indian drugs and treatments has been of enormous value.

The Virginia physicians and apothecaries during the early 1600s were often dependent upon many known Indian remedies. They searched the woods for the popular Indian medicines: hemp, tobacco, papoose root, bloodroot, dogwood, mandrake, ginseng, and wild ipecac.

The plant part most commonly used by the Indians was the root. Symbolic and revered, it represented many things to the early harvesters of botanicals. Fresh roots and herbs were chewed and often powdered and boiled with animal fat to make salves. An observer writing in the *Aborigines of Virginia* (1608) noted that they made an ointment by crushing the roots of puccoon with bear grease and ashes. This mixture was rubbed on the skin to conserve the body's heat and also to keep lice, fleas, and vermin away. Obviously, the custom of greasing the body with vegetable or animal oils helped to protect the Indians from the cold. Along with this, plants of the mint family were commonly used by the Indians to prevent and relieve insect bites, and these herbs were often mixed with bear grease. According to many early accounts, the Indians were generally free of skin diseases and maintained smooth, healthy skin by frequently "washing" the skin with the oils of fishes and the fats of eagles, raccoons, bears, and so on — mixed with certain herbs to lend fragrance and added protection.

The native Americans were experts at gathering the wild plants of their environment. They would usually dig the *roots* of annuals in early spring, before the plant flowered. The roots of biennials and perennials were most often harvested in the autumn, after the season's growth had withered, leaving these roots rich in stored nutrients before winter. *Bark* was preferably gathered in winter or early spring, when it was easiest to remove. The *leaves* of most edible herbs were gathered before their blossoming time for maximum nutrients and tenderness.

The following treatments reflect specific usage by one or more tribes. *Those marked with an asterisk (*) can be poisonous unless used in moderation.*

AMERICAN GINSENG *(Panax quinquefolius)* is a perennial woodland herb which is becoming increasingly scarce due to over-harvesting. Amerindians used a decoction of the root to settle the stomach and to relieve nausea, vomiting, and the congestion of colds. Collect the roots *sparingly,* and only when found growing in abundance. This plant is on the endangered species list in many states.

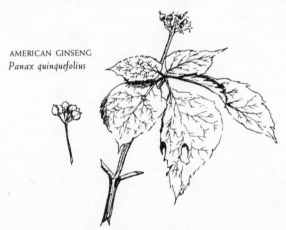

AMERICAN GINSENG
Panax quinquefolius

*AMERICAN IPECAC *(Gillenia stipulata)* and BOWMAN'S ROOT *(G. trifoliata).* These perennial North American herbs are still known as "Indian-physic." Among many tribes the raw roots were eaten in moderation as a purgative.

AMERICAN MOUNTAIN ASH *(Pirus americana)* is an indigenous, smooth-barked small tree of the rose family. The bark's chemistry is very similar to that of wild cherry, and both were used medicinally by native tribes in tonics to reduce fevers. The attractive ash berries are antiscorbutic and, when ripe, high in malic acid.

AMERICAN WHITE HELLEBORE
Veratrum viride

*AMERICAN WHITE HELLEBORE (*Veratrum viride* and 4 spp.) is a pubescent perennial wetland herb, some species of which are native to North America. *Highly poisonous*, the root was utilized as an aboriginal endurance drug. Many tribes used this botanical, in moderation, as a cardiac depressant, sedative, and internal treatment for arthritis. Certain alkaloids, acids, and mineral salts refined from the roots are used in medicine today.

AVENS, WATER (*Geum rivale*). Boiled in a strong decoction, the roots, which contain tannin, were used by many tribes to relieve sore throats and coughs, as well as a healthful dark tea to strengthen the individual against disease rashes — that is, measles, chicken pox, and smallpox.

BLACK ALDER, Winterberry, Feverbush (*Ilex verticillata*), was a noted medicinal to many tribes, who used the shrub's bark and fruit.

*BLOODROOT, or Red Puccoon (*Sanguinaria canadensis*), was a favorite Indian rheumatism remedy. The red juice of the root contains a number of alkaloids and as a tea drink was used to cure ringworm. The juice was also rubbed on the skin, not only as a brilliant dye but as an insect repellent. *Caution: This plant can have poisonous effects on the system.*

BLOODROOT
Sanguinaria canadensis

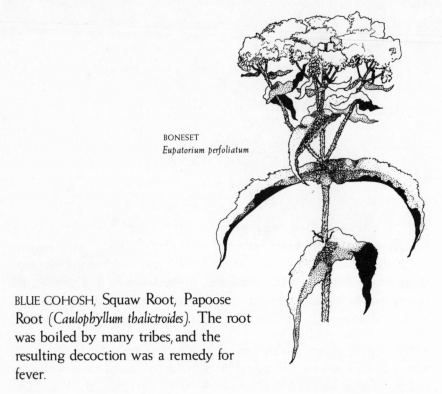

BONESET
Eupatorium perfoliatum

BLUE COHOSH, Squaw Root, Papoose Root (*Caulophyllum thalictroides*). The root was boiled by many tribes, and the resulting decoction was a remedy for fever.

BONESET or Thoroughwort (*Eupatorium perfoliatum*). Tea made from the leaves and flowers was used by the Iroquois and Mohegans as a cold remedy, to reduce fevers, and to relieve stomachaches and pain. This wide-spread herb found in wet ground and thickets was usually harvested in August for use in numerous medicines.

BORAGE (*Borago officinalis*). Tea brewed from the leaves and flowers has a natural saline content and helps to relieve fevers and cold discomforts. An herb rich in calcium and potassium, it promotes healthy tissues. Indians used borage tea externally as well as internally.

BUGLEWEED or Water Horehound (*Lycopus virginicus*) is a common perennial herb indigenous to North America in low, damp, shady areas. Medicinally it is a sedative (believed to be narcotic). A strong infusion of the leaves and stems was drunk to lower the pulse and is beneficial in the treatment of diabetes, chronic diarrhea, and dysentery.

*CATNIP (*Nepeta cataria*). This valuable, introduced herb was used extensively by the Mohegans as a medicinal tea to relieve cold symptoms and soothe colic in infants, as it has a sedative effect. The leaves and whitish flowers were harvested in August and September when in blossom and were dried before using.

CHAPARRAL, Creosote Bush, Blackbush *(Larrea tridentata)*. A strong-smelling, low shrub native to the sparsely vegetated alkaline soils of the desert and the plains of the southwestern United States, this rugged perennial was considered a veritable cure-all and was extensively used by many tribes. The dried leaves, twigs, and resinous gum were used in various preparations as an astringent, a diuretic, and a tonic for treating bruises, wounds, female disorders, kidney troubles, colds, and stomach disorders. Many Indians still sprinkle the powdered leaves inside their shoes to prevent rheumatism in their feet.

CLOVERS *(Trifolium* spp.*)* and SWEET CLOVERS *(Melilotus* spp.*)*. Early settlers and numerous Indian tribes used these sweet-scented annual/perennial herbs (many of which were naturalized in North America from abroad) in teas, additives to breads, flavorings for snuff and smoking mixtures, moth repellents, and so on. Medicinally they were a vital component in soothing salves to treat sores, ulcers and burns, and a strong infusion helped suspend coughing spasms.

CLUB-MOSSES *(Lycopodium* spp.*)*. The Blackfoot and Potawatomi tribes dusted the yellowish spores on wounds to stop bleeding. These are still used to absorb fluids from injured tissues as well as to prevent pills from sticking together in closed containers. (These same spores were also used at one time in theatrical explosives.)

COMFREY *(Symphytum officinale* and spp.*)* leaves and roots contain allantoin, a cell-proliferant, and have a long history of usage as a healing agent (both internally and externally) for broken bones and tissue damage. Introduced by the colonists to the Indians, it has known extensive use as an infusion to treat bruises, sores, insect bites, and burns. As a healthful tea it was drunk to relieve bronchial discomforts, coughs, colds, stomach disorders, and mouth sores. An infusion of comfrey leaves and roots is also soothing and beneficial in the bath water.

CORN *(Zea mays)* has impressive curative powers. It was used by the Incas and Aztecs to treat infections of the bladder and kidneys. CORN FUNGUS *(Ustilago maydis)* contains the alkaloid ustilagine (similar to ergot). Smut (predecessor of commercial penicillin) was principally used as a medicine to treat migraine headaches. Cornstarch and the smoke of burning corncobs were also used to relieve itching.

CULVER'S PHYSIC, or Culver's Root (*Veronicastrum virginicum*). A tall, graceful perennial North American herb. Many native peoples used the fresh root as a stomach tonic and laxative and to reduce fever.

DANDELION (*Taraxacum officinale*). After it was introduced to this country, the Ojibways, Mohegans, and other tribes used dandelion roots and leaves in medicinal tea decoctions for heartburn and digestive problems.

DOGWOOD (*Cornus* spp). "Hat-ta-wa-no-min-schi" is an old Indian medicine. The inner bark contains the glucoside cornin, and was boiled into a tea used as an astringent and to reduce fevers. The FLOWERING DOGWOOD (*Cornus florida*), or "Mon-ha-can-ni-min-schi" to the Delaware, was highly valued for its dense wood. The Indians also utilized its inner bark and twigs as a dentifrice, and as such these substances were both chewed and rubbed on the teeth and gums. The sturdy twigs were also carefully chewed in order to fashion natural paintbrushes. SILKY DOGWOOD (*Cornus sericea*) was known as "Milawapamule" to the Cree Indians of the Hudson Bay region. Scrapings of the wood and bark were mixed with herbs in the smoking mixture known as kinnikinnick; bark decoctions were used to treat coughs and fevers. Boiling the roots in water produced a good scarlet dye, and boiling with iron rust produced a fast black dye.

ELDERBERRY (*Sambucus canadensis*). The Iroquois boiled the inner bark and used it as a pain-killer; the dried, crushed leaves are an effective insect repellent; the flowers act as a stimulant and induce sweating.

EYEBRIGHT (*Euphrasia americana* and spp.) is a common low-growing annual herb, indigenous to open fields. Many cultures brewed a tea from the whole, fresh flowering plant that was used both externally and internally, primarily for ophthalmic disorders.

FEVERROOT, Horse Gentian, Wild Coffee (*Triosteum perfoliatum* and spp.). These coarse, leafy perennials indigenous to North America favor the open woodlands and limestone soils. The Cherokees brewed a decoction of the dark green leaves as a febrifuge. The dried roasted nutlets were (and are) an excellent coffee beverage. The Onondagas prepared poultices of the roots to treat swellings and to reduce inflammation and external pain.

GOLDENROD (*Solidago* spp.) blossoms were chewed by the Zunis to alleviate sore throats.

GROUND IVY, Gill-over-the-ground, Fieldbalm, Cat's-foot (*Nepeta hederacea*). An introduced member of the mint family, ground ivy was brewed and steeped as a cooling tea and external poultice.

HEAL-ALL, Selfheal, Carpenter-weed (*Prunella vulgaris*). Like its relative, ground ivy, this widely dispersed native member of the mint family was used as a cooling tea and poultice.

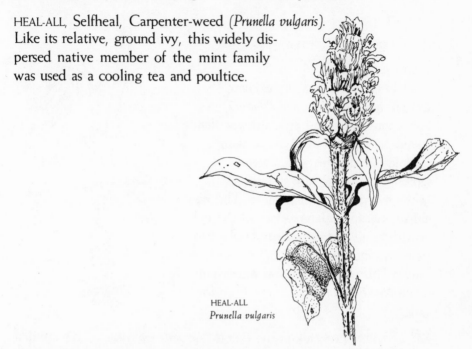

HEAL-ALL
Prunella vulgaris

HEMLOCK (*Tsuga canadensis*) has great nutritional value, and its tannin-rich bark was used in tanning animal hides. This native evergreen was used extensively by the Penobscot, Micmac, and Montagnais tribes as a tea to relieve colds, and a medicinal bath was prepared of the steeped branches. The Menominees and Forest Potawatomis also used hemlock tea to treat colds, to induce sweating, and to reduce fevers. Beds of hemlock branches refreshed their tired hunters and renewed their strength.

HOPS, or Common Hops (*Humulus lupulus*). This perennial, native of the Northern Hemisphere, was used medicinally as a tonic, febrifuge, and sedative. Since antiquity, hops have been used in brewing to preserve and to add a wholesome bitterness to the resulting liquid.

ICELAND MOSS lichen (*Cetraria islandica*) makes an excellent medicinal tea used to dissolve mucus congestion. Boil 1 teaspoon of the dried, powdered plant in 1 cup water for 30 minutes; strain and sweeten. Take one or two cupfuls daily.

INDIAN PIPE
Monotropa uniflora

INDIAN PIPE, Pinesap, Corpse Plant, Convulsion-root *(Monotropa uniflora)*, is indigenous to beech-dominant woodlands. Found growing on dead or decaying organic matter, this widespread saprophyte flowers July through September after soaking rains. The noted Indian cure for inflammations of the eye involved pulverizing the whole plant to clear, glutinous fluid and mixing with water. This was also used as a soothing treatment for other irritations, even for epilepsy.

*INDIAN TURNIP, or Jack-in-the-Pulpit *(Arisaema triphyllum)*. This familiar woodland perennial wild flower was used by numerous tribes as a headache treatment. The toxic root, containing the acrid poison calcium oxalate, was pounded with water into a pulp, then allowed to dry several weeks (rendering it harmless). In this state it was used variously as a palatable flour, as snuff, and as a medicinal tea.

INDIGO or Rattleweed *(Baptisia tinctoria)*. A slender, branching perennial herb indigenous to the Northern Hemisphere, indigo has been used for centuries as a dye and drug: many tribes used its roots and stems as an "antiseptic" dressing for wounds and as a treatment for typhoid fever.

JEWELWEED or Touch-me-not *(Impatiens* spp.*)* is the common succulent weed often found growing in or near poison ivy. Considered nature's antidote, the clear plant juice of the jewelweed stems and leaves was a widely used Indian remedy for external poison ivy rash and eczema. In order to be effective it must be applied soon after contact.

JUNIPER *(Juniperus communis)*. Oil from the crushed berries was rubbed on the skin as an insect repellent. The stems, leaves, and berries were also brewed into a warming tea to drink or to use as an astringent. The berries and inner bark are excellent survival foods. Indians also burned the bark and branches of juniper and cedar and bathed in their healing smoke beside the warming fire. They also used the smoke to purify the air inside their dwellings.

LICORICE *(Glycyrrhiza glabra)*. The leaves were brewed to a strong, warm tea, which was used as an external treatment for earache. Licorice root was used as a laxative and as a flavoring in medicines.

*LOBELIA or Indian Tobacco *(Lobelia inflata* and spp.)*. The leaves were dried and smoked (in moderation) as a popular asthma remedy. *Caution: This plant can be poisonous if used in quantity.*

*MAY APPLE, Mandrake, Wild Jalap *(Podophyllum peltatum)*. *Poisonous* in large doses because it contains harmful alkaloids, may apple was used as an Indian suicide drug. In small quantities the root was used as a cathartic. It was also pulverized by the Penobscots as a treatment for warts and skin eruptions.

*MILKWEED *(Asclepias syriaca)*. Latex was a specific Indian skin treatment for ringworm and warts.

*MULLEIN *(Verbascum thapsus)*. Leaves and roots were dried and used in a variety of ways for respiratory problems. The Mohegans steeped the leaves in water and molasses to make a good cough remedy. Steeped longer, until very thick, the "candied" syrup can be dried into lozenges to treat mouth and throat sores. The Catawbas, Penobscots, Mohegans, and Forest Potowatomis used it in this manner. Many cultures smoked the dried mullein leaves to relieve the symptoms of asthma.

JEWELWEED
Impatiens biflora

MUSTARDS *(Brassica* spp.) are a large family of pungent, coarse, hairy herbs, naturalized on our continent from Europe and the Orient. They have escaped cultivation for long enough to be considered "common weeds." Indians used mustards as medicines, cosmetics, foods, and condiments. WILD BLACK MUSTARD *(Brassica nigra)* is the principal source of table mustard; its black seeds are used as food seasonings. The young leaves of WHITE MUSTARD *(Brassica hirta)* may be used in salads; its pale seeds are used for flavoring.

NANNYBERRY, Sheepberry, Wild Raisin *(Viburnum lentago).* The bark has many medicinal uses; gather it in spring as the shrub flowers; dry and store for later use. For an infusion to relieve cramps and abdominal distress, steep 1 ounce finely powdered bark in 1 pint boiling water until cool. Strain and take 1 teaspoonful three times a day, before each meal.

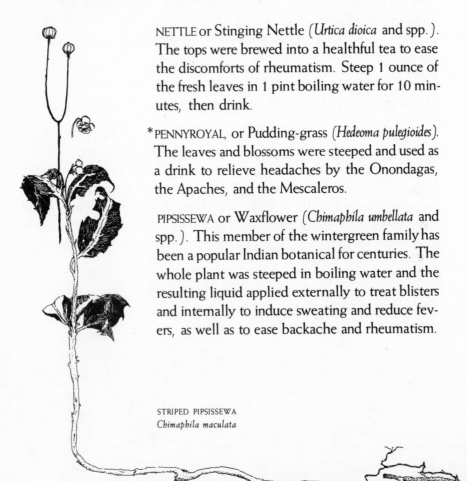

NETTLE or Stinging Nettle *(Urtica dioica* and spp.). The tops were brewed into a healthful tea to ease the discomforts of rheumatism. Steep 1 ounce of the fresh leaves in 1 pint boiling water for 10 minutes, then drink.

*PENNYROYAL, or Pudding-grass *(Hedeoma pulegioides).* The leaves and blossoms were steeped and used as a drink to relieve headaches by the Onondagas, the Apaches, and the Mescaleros.

PIPSISSEWA or Waxflower *(Chimaphila umbellata* and spp.). This member of the wintergreen family has been a popular Indian botanical for centuries. The whole plant was steeped in boiling water and the resulting liquid applied externally to treat blisters and internally to induce sweating and reduce fevers, as well as to ease backache and rheumatism.

STRIPED PIPSISSEWA
Chimaphila maculata

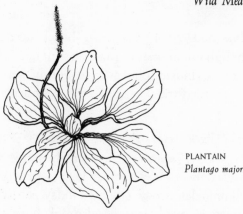

PLANTAIN
Plantago major

PLANTAIN or White Man's Foot *(Plantago major* and *P. lanceolata)* leaves were heated by the Shoshoni Indians and applied as a wet dressing to wounds. The root was chewed to relieve toothache and mouth sores. The whole plant was macerated and used as an antidote to reptile and insect bites. The seeds were used as a remedy for worms.

PLUM or Wild Plum *(Prunus americana).* The inner bark was scraped and boiled, and this decoction was then gargled and held in the mouth briefly to cure sores of the mouth and throat.

*POKEWEED or Pigeonberry *(Phytolacca americana)* was commonly utilized by the native Americans as a medicine, dye, ink, and spring potherb. Virginia tribes boiled the toxic berries in a tea to cure rheumatism. Concoctions of poke root were applied externally for various skin diseases and parasites. *Caution: This plant can be poisonous.*

SASSAFRAS *(Sassafras albidum).* The roots were boiled into a strong tea to treat fevers. The young sprouts were boiled to make an eyewash.

SENECA SNAKEROOT *(Polygala senega).* The old generic name of this indigenous shrub is derived from the Seneca Indians' noted use of this plant. Several Indian tribes used it to treat snake and animal bites, pneumonia, asthma, and rheumatism. An infusion of the leaves was also effective in the treatment of eye inflammations.

SASSAFRAS
Sassafras albidum

SKULLCAP *(Scutellaria lateriflora* and spp.). Common bitter perennial herbs of the mint family, though not aromatic, these ancient native botanicals were utilized by numerous Indian tribes as tonics for the nervous system. Their most unique recorded tribal usage was in treatments for tetanus and rabies.

SPRUCE, WHITE, or Cat Spruce *(Picea glauca)*. Along with the RED SPRUCE *(P. rubens)* and BLACK or BOG SPRUCE *(P. mariana)*, these stately native trees provide an impressive pharmacopeia of uses. Spruce beer is an original Indian formula to prevent vitamin deficiency, still used today. The twigs and cones of spruce are boiled in maple syrup and drunk hot, year-round. This delicious brew early became an important American folk medicine.

SQUASH and PUMPKIN *(Cucurbita* spp.) and GOURD *(Lagenaria* spp.). The dried seeds were chewed as worm expellents.

GOURD SEEDS
Lagenaria siceraria

STONEROOT or Horse Balm *(Collinsonia canadensis)*. This large-leafed, strong-scented eastern North American perennial favors rich woodlands. Most eastern tribes used it as a medical panacea. A strong tea relieved headaches, cramps, indigestion, fevers, dropsy. It was also considered a stimulant and used to treat diseases of the respiratory tract, especially asthma; in addition, many tribes prepared poultices of the leaves and yellow blossoms to treat sores, wounds, bruises, and hemorrhoids.

SWEET FERN or Meadow Fern *(Comptonia peregrina)* is an indigenous, low shrub of the bayberry family *(Myricaceae)* and not a fern at all. Favoring open woodlands and clearings, and relatively sterile soil, this lacy-leafed shrub was sought for its very fragrant foliage. Its leaves and flowering tips were brewed into a nurturing tea, to treat diarrhea and other stomach disorders. The volatile oils from the crushed leaves act as insect repellents when rubbed on the skin. These fresh leaves are an especially effective poison-ivy antidote when applied to the skin immediately after contact.

*TANSY, Common Tansy, Gold Buttons (*Tanacetum vulgare*) of escaped European heritage, and *T. huronense,* a native herb indigenous to our Great Lakes regions, have centuries of annotated historical uses. Its resinous leaves and flowers were used externally to kill fleas and lice, and internally to treat worms. A warming tea was brewed to be used mainly in treating skin conditions. *Caution: Tansy taken internally can be fatal.*

TOBACCO (*Nicotiana* spp.). The leaves, when chewed, were a favorite Indian bee sting remedy and an insect repellent. The dried, powdered leaves are still an effective insect repellent. Tobacco smoking was used as a sedative and considered very relaxing to tired limbs.

VALERIAN (*Valeriana* spp.) is a hardy family of native (and introduced) perennial herbs. The odorous roots were often used as an antispasmodic and act as a strong sedative. The leaves were used in preparations for wounds. Because of this plant's high silica content and natural phosphorus, it makes a fine antiseptic.

WATERMELON (*Citrullus lanatus*). The dried seeds were used as a treatment for kidney and circulatory conditions.

WHITE OAK (*Quercus alba*). The inner bark was collected during the spring, when it was highest in tannic acid content; washed and brewed into a warming tea, it was used by many tribes to cure diarrhea and piles. The Mohegans used the bark as a cold remedy.

WHITE PINE (*Pinus strobus*) was extensively used by many Indians. New England tribes boiled the needles in water or maple syrup and drank this tea to prevent scurvy and to relieve coughs and colds. These needles contain five times more vitamin C than an equal amount of lemons, and they are also a rich source of vitamin A. Just chewing the freshly picked needles is very beneficial. The Objibway Indians used the seeds to flavor their cooking. The Iroquois Indians ate the sweet inner bark.

WHITE PINE
Pinus strobus

WHITE POPLAR or Silver Poplar *(Populus alba)*. The inner bark has properties similar to willow bark.

WILD BERGAMOT *(Monarda fistulosa)*. Extracted from the dried, boiled leaves, bergamot oil (which contains thymol) was used by numerous tribes to treat cold symptoms and bronchitis. This volatile oil is a stimulant and may be used to relieve stomach gases.

WILD GERANIUM
Geranium maculatum

WILD GERANIUM *(Geranium maculatum)*. The roots were gathered in the autumn, when their nutritive content was highest, then boiled with wild grape to make a liquid gargle for sores of the mouth and throat. This common native spring-blossoming wildflower was effectively used by a number of tribes. High in tannin, the dried, powdered roots were also used as a dressing to stop bleeding.

WILD LETTUCE *(Lactuca* spp). Its milky juices were used by the Menominees on poison-ivy rash; it was also used in medicines for its hypnotic, sedative, and diuretic properties.

WILD ONION *(Allium cernuum* and spp.) The whole plant was used as an insect repellent and was rubbed all over the body.

WILD SARSAPARILLA *(Aralia nudicaulis* and spp.). The rootstock was dried and pulverized for medicinal teas, which were taken internally to treat colds and the effects of rheumatism, and applied externally for skin disorders. Infusion: Steep 1 teaspoon dried rootstock in 1 cup boiling water for 10 minutes. Drink 1 or 2 cupfuls daily.

WILLOW *(Salix* spp.*).* The inner bark contains the glucoside salicin, a primitive form of aspirin (which is acetylsalicylic acid). This prolific species was extensively used for many centuries by most North American tribes. The inner bark was used in Indian steam baths, to relieve rheumatic discomforts. Willow root and bark teas were brewed and drunk to relieve pain and to reduce fevers.

WINTERGREEN, Checkerberry, Teaberry *(Gaultheria procumbens).* The evergreen leaves and red berries, prepared in tea infusions, were used for centuries by the Indians as an astringent, diuretic, stimulant, febrifuge, and pain-killer. A poultice of wintergreen was also used to relieve rheumatic pains. Oil of wintergreen — methyl salicylate — is still used commercially to flavor other medicines.

WITCH HAZEL *(Hamamelis virginiana),* an indigenous shrub of the moist woodlands, is an ancient Indian antiseptic, widely used by many tribes as an astringent wash on wounds, bruises, and muscular aches. The shiny black seeds are edible, and the Iroquois made a warming tea of the sweetened boiled leaves.

*WORMWOOD or Prairie Sagewort *(Artemisia frigida).* An indigenous perennial herb with the fragrance of sage, wormwood was used as a source of camphor by many tribes. A tea of the boiled leaves was a noted treatment for bronchitis, sore throat, and colds.

*YARROW or Milfoil *(Achillea millefolium.)* The root was used by the Zuni Indians as a local anesthetic and antiseptic wash for wounds and ears. The chewed leaves were used to reduce swelling around wounds and to deaden toothache. Oil of yarrow (cineol) is a cooling, soothing treatment for burns; it was also used among many Indian tribes to prevent falling hair but was especially a noted contraceptive and abortive. The leaves steeped in water are a good styptic. Caution: Extended use can cause sensitivity.

XI
❖
WILD SMOKING MIXTURES

American Indians introduced the early settlers to smoking, which they used both medicinally and ceremonially. Pipes were most often used, although some tribes prepared and smoked cornhusk cigarettes.

The Indians' life-styles revolved around their cooking and habitation fires, and smoke was an important part of daily life. Specific types of twigs, wood, and pine cones were burned at certain times for their fragrances and for curing food. Soothing types of smoke were also used to bathe the body.

The Indians smoked a variety of dried wild herbs, blended with a very small amount of tobacco. Consequently, the nicotine content of their smoking materials was minor. By contrast, modern smoking materials use more flavorful tobacco, rolled in chemically treated papers to assist burning and to prevent flavor loss, and the nicotine content is considerable. It is valuable to note that the American Indians also used tobacco as a sacrificial offering, a medicine, and an effective insecticide (nicotine, $C_{10}H_{14}N_2$, is a poisonous alkaloid). Aside from the native tobacco, *Nicotiana rustica* and *N. tobacum*, the Indians smoked an impressive assortment of botanicals, many of which are still available at tobacconists today because of their beneficial qualities.

Those smoking substances marked with an asterisk (*) can be poisonous unless used in moderation.

ANGELICA
Angelica atropurpurea

ANGELICA or "La-go-nee-ham" (*Angelica atropurpurea*) has a fragrant odor and a warm, aromatic taste. Many tribes prized the dried leaves as a fine smoking commodity alone or mixed them with tobacco. This was also a favored ingredient in the medicine bag.

BEARBERRY, Kinnikinnick, Mealberry, Upland Cranberry (*Arctostyphylos uva-ursi*) is an evergreen member of the heath family. This trailing shrub has papery reddish bark and small paddle-shaped leaves. The Indian term for it originally meant a smoking mixture including sumac bark, native tobacco, spicebush, and bearberry. However, this low-growing plant became so popular as a smoke by itself that *kinnikinnick* came to refer to it specifically. The Chippewas mixed bearberry leaves with tobacco and red willow as a medicinal smoke to relieve headaches. The Potowatomis mixed bearberry with tobacco for a mild smoking blend. The early French settlers were especially fond of smoking bearberry leaves.

BRISTLY CROWFOOT (*Ranunculus pensylvanicus*) is indigenous to wetlands across America. The fruiting heads, seeds, and leaflets were harvested in autumn for smoking mixtures.

BUTTERWEED or Horse-weed (*Erigeron canadensis*) is a widespread native of the composite family. It was favored for its flowers and bristly leaves by numerous Indian tribes.

COLTSFOOT *(Tussilago farfara)*, European-introduced; and SWEET COLTS-FOOT *(Petasites palmata* and spp.), native. These perennial woolly boreal herbs of damp woodlands were sought for their broad leaves. Aside from seasonings, the dried leaves were enjoyed as a tobacco, providing relief for sore throats.

CORN *(Zea mays)*. Cornsilk, the fine, yellowish, silky threads of the stigmas from the female flowers of maize, was dried and rolled into cornhusk cigarettes by certain tribes.

DITTANY or "Mas-tin-jay" *(Cunila origanoides)* is a native perennial of the mint family. Its smooth, fragrant leaves were prized for smoking and chewing by numerous tribes.

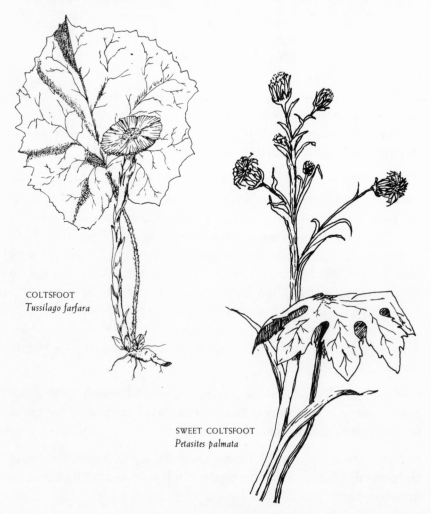

COLTSFOOT
Tussilago farfara

SWEET COLTSFOOT
Petasites palmata

FIELD MINT *(Mentha* spp.*)* was smoked alone or mixed with other herbs. The dried leaves are a flavorful and soothing tobacco.

GOLDENROD *(Solidago* spp.*).* The fragrant flowers and leaves were enjoyed as a medicinal smoke by the Ojibwas, who also used this as a hunting smoke to attract deer.

LICORICE *(Glycyrrhiza glabra)* has good keeping qualities. Because of its flavor and medicinal properties it was frequently mixed with other herbal tobaccos.

LIFE EVERLASTING *(Gnaphalium polycephalum)* and PEARLY EVERLASTING *(Anaphalis margaritacea)* were valued Indian herbs. They were chewed to relieve hoarseness and irritations of the mouth and throat. Indian medicine men carried this fragrant herb, claiming that the leaves cleared and strengthened the voice and provoked the "urge to sing." It is a favorite pipe smoke, having a fragrance similar to hickory, and a good substitute for the tobacco-chewing habit. Indians also smoked this herb to relieve headaches.

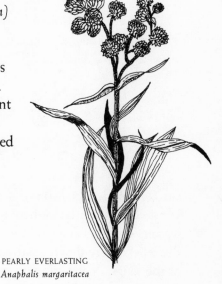

PEARLY EVERLASTING
Anaphalis margaritacea

*LOBELIA or Indian Tobacco *(Lobelia inflata* and spp.*).* Use with caution. This indigenous "wild tobacco" is a branching annual herb. The leaves of this plant were dried and used by many Indian tribes, principally as a stimulant and expectorant. It was a popular asthma remedy; however, taking too much of this plant induces coma and causes death. Lobelia contains the alkaloid lobeline, which, like nicotine, acts first as a stimulant and then as a depressant on the autonomic nerves. This alkaloid is used in a number of antismoking preparations because it induces nausea.

MEADOWSWEET *(Spiraea alba* and spp.*).* This multi-useful perennial was favored by many tribes and as pipestem wood by the Chippewas.

MULLEIN
Verbascum thapsus

*MULLEIN *(Verbascum thapsus)* is a common biennial cosmopolitan herb whose leaves can be gathered and dried any time during the growing season. The American Indians smoked the dried leaves in their pipes for the relief of sore throats, asthma, coughs, congestion, and inflammation of the lungs. Many tribes made a sweetened infusion of the leaves and roots for use in relieving these same symptoms in children.

NEW ENGLAND ASTER *(Aster novae-angliae* and spp.) and other woodland and meadow asters. The roots and blossoms were dried and powdered to be used as smoking tobacco. The Ojibways favored these lovely plants as a hunting smoke to attract deer, and they used asters for food and medicinals.

PANICLED DOGWOOD *(Cornus racemosa* and spp.), RED OSIER DOGWOOD *(Cornus stolonifera* and spp.), and other indigenous shrubs of the dogwood family, were sought year-round, especially for their inner bark, which was dried, ground fine, and added to smoking mixtures.

PARTRIDGEBERRY or Squaw Vine *(Mitchella repens)*, the low-growing woodland evergreen, was harvested principally by the Chippewas for smoking and was used also as a food and a medicinal.

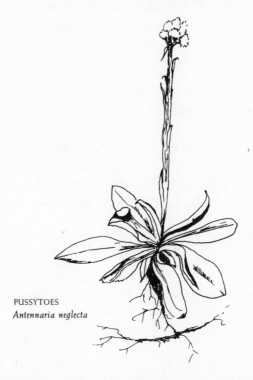

PUSSYTOES
Antennaria neglecta

PUSSYTOES (*Antennaria neglecta* and spp.) became known as Ladies' Tobacco. This small, widespread cosmopolitan weed was enjoyed as a fine smoking plant by many northeastern tribes. The diminutive gray-green plant has white to pink flowers in April and May. Both its blossoms and its leaves were dried and used.

SASSAFRAS(*Sassafras albidum* and spp.). Known to the Indians as "Shikih," this plant was well prized for its many uses. The Indians smoked the spicy, aromatic bark of the dried root like tobacco.

SMOOTH SUMAC (*Rhus glabra*) and STAGHORN SUMAC (*Rhus typhina* and spp.). The fuzzy red berries, harvested in the autumn, were cured by drying and were enjoyed alone as a healthful smoke or in mixtures of the dried sumac leaves and roots. Called "Kinikah" by the Plains Indians, sumac was also smoked along with dried tobacco leaves.

According to the *Historical Dictionary of 1813*, sumac berries became so esteemed in Europe for smoking that they were preferred to the best cured Virginia tobacco.

SUNFLOWER (*Helianthus* spp.). The leaves were dried and used as a tobacco substitute in cigars and pipes.

SWEET CLOVER (*Melilotus* spp.). The blossoms and leaves of about twenty species of wild clovers were dried and used to flavor tobacco smoking mixtures.

*TOBACCO (*Nicotiana* spp.) were sacred plants. The dried leaves were given as offerings before wild herbs were harvested or certain animals hunted. Also, the cured leaves were used in tribal council meetings and in religious ceremonies. Upward-drifting smoke was thought to carry messages to the Sky-World above, thus enabling the Indians to communicate with the Creator and ancestral spirits. Tobacco smoking was also considered calming to the spirit and relaxing for the body.

*WILD LETTUCE (*Lactuca virosa* and spp.) was dried and smoked to calm the nerves.

*WOOLLY YARROW (*Achillea lanulosa* and spp.). Yarrow was a favored native smoking commodity. This plant contains cineol, a dark blue volatile oil that is stimulating and cooling.

XII

NATURAL CHEWING GUMS

Many plants and trees exude sap, latex, or resinous material that contain essential nutrients as well as natural sugars. Indians prized many different substances as "chewing gums," and Indian children made games out of seeking these out. Often, simply chewing on several fresh pine needles until their sweet and sour essences were extracted was enough to satisfy thirst and relieve hunger pains. They were also a source of vitamin C and a soothing treatment for mouth sores, sore throats, and coughs. Other "chewing gums" were used to relieve toothache, headache, and indigestion. Favored substances included the following:

BALSAM FIR (*Abies balsamea*), as well as many other members of the pine family, exudes a resinous pitch from the trunk and twigs when wounded. This pitch is chewy and delicious raw, sticky to relatively firm when aged. The Indians heightened its piny taste by heating the pitch over a fire until it bubbled and crystallized.

BLACK BIRCH BARK (*Betula lenta*) was carefully peeled, and small pieces were enjoyed raw or boiled for several minutes and then chewed. This gum provides refreshing and beneficial juices. *Caution:* Peeling away much of the outer bark will kill the tree.

CHICORY
Cichorium intybus

BLUE LETTUCE (*Lactuca pulchella*) was used by the Zunis, who cut the roots of the young plants and dried the exuded milky latex for chewing gum.

CHARCOAL from wood fires was used among most tribes to whiten and clean teeth, sweeten the breath, and relieve stomach gas. The natural tendency of charcoal is to absorb gases and purify substances.

CHICORY roots (*Cichorium intybus*) were chewed fresh by many tribes; they are fibrous, spongy, and nutritious.

CLEMATIS (*Clematis verticillaris* and spp.) was sought for its slightly woody stems and bitter-sweet plant juices.

DANDELION roots (*Taraxacum officinale*) were used much the same as fresh chicory roots, but their dried latex was especially prized as a chewing substance.

DOGWOOD twigs and bark (*Cornus* spp.) were used as a dentrifrice. The young twigs were peeled and the ends chewed to make paintbrushes, as well as to scrub and clean the teeth and gums.

HAWKWEED roots (*Hieracium canadense* and spp.) were chewed in summer to relieve thirst.

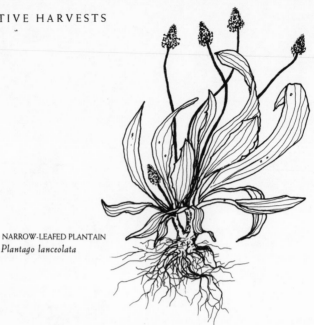

NARROW-LEAFED PLANTAIN
Plantago lanceolata

HOLLYHOCK *(Althaea rosea)* was favored for its peeled, fresh stems, which were chewed in small chunks.

INDIAN HEMP *(Apocynum cannabinum* and spp.) was sought most notably for cordage fibers, but its milky, sticky latex was chewed as gum by the Kiowas, Shoshones, and numerous other tribes.

LARKSPUR LETTUCE *(Lactuca ludoviciana)*, as well as numerous other species of wild lettuce, was used like the Blue Lettuce.

LICORICE roots *(Glycyrrhiza glabra)* were esteemed as chewing substances in small pieces.

MARSHMALLOW *(Althaea officinalis)* was sought for centuries for its roots, which yielded the mucilaginous paste that was the original source of today's popular confection.

MILKWEED *(Asclepias syriaca* and spp.) exudes a milky, sticky latex which was chewed as gum by the Kiowas and Shoshones.

PLANTAIN roots *(Plantago major* and *P. lanceolata)* were chewed especially to relieve toothache and thirst.

PUSSYTOES *(Antennaria neglecta* and spp.). Its roots and silvery-gray leaves were chewed.

REED GRASS *(Phragmites communis)*. Stalks were punctured, and the exuded pasty, sugary substance was hardened into gum. Indians collected this and compressed it into balls to be chewed as desired or toasted near the fire until brown, to be eaten like taffy.

SALSIFY or Oyster Plant *(Tragopogon porrifolius)*. The peeled stems and roots were chewed, in chunks, and the nutritious juices swallowed to relieve indigestion.

SPRUCE *(Picea rubens* and spp.*)*. The hardened exuded sap of these trees was aged 3 days, or more, before chewing.

SUGAR PINE *(Pinus lambertiana)* exudes a sugary, brown, gummy sap that is excellent for chewing.

SWEET GUM or RED GUM *(Liquidambar styraciflua)* is the source of the exuded resin gum copal, which is a pleasant chewing gum.

WHITE PINE *(Pinus strobus)* exudes a sticky amber sap that is very favorable for chewing.

Aside from the botanicals mentioned here, there are countless additional substances in nature that may be similarly used. Besides saps, resins, roots, and peeled stems of botanicals, the Indians also used many leaves and blossoms of herbs as seasonal chewing material. Principal among these was tobacco, which was chewed by many Indian peoples.

SALSIFY
Tragopogon porrifolius

XIII

❖

POISONOUS WILD PLANTS

nly a small portion of the thousands of species of wild plants are dangerously poisonous. Certain other plants are toxic to the human system and can cause disturbing side effects but are not fatal if ingested. For safety's sake, keep the following guidelines in mind:

- Never use any plant that you cannot specifically identify as edible, especially berries, shoots, roots, and mushrooms. *Mistakes can be fatal!*
- Animals are *not* reliable indicators of edibility.
- Learn to recognize common poisonous plants and avoid them.
- Learn to identify plants that cause dermatitis and learn to recognize their natural antidotes. Jewelweed stems and leaves relieve the effects of poison ivy, while plantain leaves relieve the effects of stinging nettles.
- Teach children to avoid dangerous wild plants. Indeed, many common houseplants are poisonous.
- Be certain about which plant parts to harvest and their proper season. Some plants are delicious young but toxic at maturity; for example, wild asparagus, poke (shoots), milkweed (shoots and leaves), and so on. Other plants are edible when sufficiently cooked

POKEWEED
Phytolacca americana

but poisonous raw; for example, Jack-in-the-pulpit (roots), marsh marigold (leaves), young poke (spears), and unripe bittersweet (berries).

· Some plants are toxic if eaten in excess, because they are much higher in vitamins and minerals than our normal hybrid vegetables and therefore rougher on the average human system.

· Do not collect contaminated plants, especially ones growing by road margins (because of the buildup of toxic substances, primarily lead from exhaust fumes). Avoid plants growing in brackish or contaminated water. Be sure the plants you gather have not been sprayed recently with insecticides or growth retardants.

· *Never use anything you are unsure of.*

· *Sample your wild harvest sparingly.* Plant and body chemistries vary from individual to individual.

· Certain poisonous plants had significant technological uses to many Indian tribes. The highly poisonous Indian hemp or dogbane (*Apocynum* spp.) is easily confused in its early growth with the edible young common milkweed. Though the first two are definitely *inedible,* they were prized (at maturity) as fiber and cordage materials.

Many tribes utilized the turkey mullein (*Croton setigerus*), known as fish-weed, and the nuts of the red buckeye (*Aesculus pavia*). These botanical poisons were pulverized and spread on the surface of pools to paralyze fish. The dazed fish would float up to the surface and could be harvested easily and eaten without apparent harm to the human system. This type of local paralysis was usually temporary, and the fish could soon be revived in fresh water. Hundreds of pounds of fish could · be caught easily by this method.

YARROW
Achillea millefolium

Yarrow (*Achillea millefolium*) is a wild herb whose flower clusters and lacy leaves may be used *in moderation*, but these plant parts contain a volatile oil that can react adversely in the human system. However, noted Indian usage of this plant was widespread. Chewing one or more (up to thirteen) feathery leaves and spitting them out after thorough chewing numbed the mouth. This was an adequate local anesthetic for toothache and tooth extraction.

It is essential to understand that plants and mushrooms have their own individuality. It is comparatively easy to assimilate the necessary knowledge to use plants properly, and it is vital to know which ones must be avoided.

The native Americans had an extensive knowledge of the poisonous and edible wild, and they utilized this information brilliantly. To a large extent this was also true of the Europeans who migrated to the North American continent, bringing with them their most important botanicals. The blending of these traditions continues to aid our understanding of the natural and cultivated worlds.

GLOSSARY

algae: Non-flowering plants, mostly aquatic, which undergo photosynthesis.

alkaloid: An organic substance having alkaline properties and containing nitrogen; such substances extracted from plants and used in certain drugs — for example, caffeine, morphine, cocaine, quinine. Some alkaloids are highly poisonous.

Amerindian: A contraction of American Indian.

annual: A plant that completes its life cycle in a single year.

antiscorbutic: A botanical that contains significant amounts of vitamin C. A remedy for scurvy.

antiseptic: A substance that destroys the microorganisms that cause infection.

aromatic: A substance with a spicy scent and pungent, pleasing taste.

astringent: A substance that causes tissues to shrink or pucker; a styptic, for example, alum.

biennial: A plant that completes its life cycle in two years, producing seeds in its second year.

botanical: Any wild or cultivated plant that has specific usefulness to man.

cambium: A layer of tissue between the inner bark and the wood of a tree, gorged with sap, sugars, and starches; a good, nutritious food source from some trees.

cardiac: An agent that has an effect on the heart.

cathartic: A strong purgative; a laxative, for example, the daylily or castor oil.

citric acid: A white, crystalline, sharply sour compound, $C_6H_8O_7$, contained in various fruits and also made synthetically.

conifer A cone-bearing plant producing naked seeds.

cultigen: A domesticated plant species of unknown or obscure origin, distinct in its characteristics from known natural species: distinguished from indigenous.

cultivar: A specially cultivated horticultural or garden variety of plant, flower, etc.

deciduous: A plant that sheds its leaves annually.

decoction: A preparation made by boiling herbs in water for a specific period of time; usually hard materials (roots, barks, and seeds) require this type of preparation. Generally, boil 1 ounce botanical in 1 pint cold water in a covered container (preferably glass or enamel) for 30 minutes. Strain and cool.

dermatitis: Inflammation and irritation of the skin, for example, poison-ivy and stinging-nettle rashes.

diuretic: An herb or medicine that causes an increase in the flow of urine.

emetic: A substance that causes vomiting, for example, ipecac.

emollient: A substance applied externally to soften and soothe the skin.

ethnobotany: A culture's use of its floral environment.

evergreen: A plant that remains green throughout the year.

expectorant: A remedy that loosens phlegm so that it may be easily brought up and expectorated.

extract: A substance refined through heat and evaporation to yield its essence, for example, maple sugar.

febrifuge: A remedy that reduces fever.

fiddlehead: The coiled or curled young shoot or frond of a fern.

floral: Adjective from flora. The aggregate of plants indigenous to a country or district: distinguished from fauna.

folic acid: An orange-yellow crystalline compound, $C_{19}H_{19}N_7O_6$, having vitaminlike properties and included in the vitamin B complex. It is found in green leaves, mushrooms, brewer's yeast, and some animal tissues and is used in the treatment of anemic conditions.

fomentation: A local application of cloths wrung out in hot water, with or without medicinals added.

frond: A fern leaf; the leaflike portion of seaweed.

fruit: Mature ovary of a flower containing one or more seeds; including berries, nuts, and grains.

fungi: A group of organisms lacking chlorophyll.

fungicide: A substance that destroys fungi.

grain: Fruits peculiar to members of the grass family; they are small and dry and contain a single seed.

gruel: A thin, easily digested broth made by cooking cornmeal in water or milk.

herb: A plant that has special usefulness as a medicine, seasoning, or flavoring.

horticulture: The cultivation of a garden.

hybrid: Produced by interbreeding or cross-fertilization. An animal or plant of mixed parentage.

hygroscopic: A substance with the ability to absorb moisture from the surrounding environment, for example, honey.

infusion: A tea made usually of the softer plant parts (blossoms and leaves). Generally, pour 1 pint boiling water over 1 ounce botanical; cover and steep for 15 minutes; strain and use. Infusions are never boiled.

intertidal: The area of the continental shelf between the high- and low-tide marks.

laxative: A substance that causes the bowels to act.

macerate: To make soft or tender, usually by soaking.

malic acid: A deliquescent crystalline acid, $C_4H_6O_5$, with a pleasant taste. Contained in the juice of many fruits, especially apples.

mucilaginous: Slimy or mucilage-like; some mucilaginous plants, such as aloe and sassafras, have a soothing quality when applied externally.

mushroom: The fruiting body of a fleshy fungus.

narcotic: Any substance that produces a depressive effect on the central nervous system.

nut: A fruit with a hard, stony, or woody shell surrounding the seed.

perennial: A plant that lives from year to year and does not die after flowering.

petiole: The stalk to which the leaf is attached.

pistil: Female part of the flower.

potage: A soup or broth.

potherb: Any wild edible plant used as food or as a flavoring.

poultice: A surface preparation to remedy skin disorders. Fresh leaves are generally used; they are crushed and steeped in boiling water for a short time, then applied with moist heat to draw or soothe.

purgative: A physic; a substance that cleanses or purges.

rhizome: A horizontal underground stem, enlarged by food storage, for example, gingerroot.

rootstock: A rhizome or subterranean stem.

saprophyte: A plant (usually lacking chlorophyll) that lives on dead organic matter, for example, the fungi.

sedative: A substance that calms the nerves.

spore print: Made by cutting off the pileus (cap) of a ripe mushroom and placing it with gills down on clean white paper; cover with an inverted glass or bowl and allow time for the spores to drop onto the paper (from two to eight hours).

stamen: The male, pollen-bearing part of a flower.

subtidal: Below the tide mark.

tincture: An alcoholic solution of medicinal substances, usually 50 percent alcohol. Generally, mix 4 ounces water and 12 ounces spirits with 1 ounce powdered herb. Seal and let stand for 2 weeks; shake the container daily. Strain and bottle the clear liquid for use. Tinctures are made with plants whose active substances are not soluble in water.

tisane: An infusion of flowers.

tonic: A drug or medicine that improves the body tone; a substance that invigorates the system.

tuber: A swollen end of an underground stem that serves as a storage organ, for example, potatoes.

viscid: Covered with a glutinous, sticky layer.

weed: Any plant that grows where it is not wanted, especially one that crowds out more desirable species in cultivated areas.

REFERENCE GUIDE
Books, Articles, Films, People

Cookbooks

Beard, James. *New Fish Cookery*. Boston and Toronto: Little, Brown & Co., 1976.

Booth, Sally S. *Hung, Strung and Potted: A History of Eating Habits in Colonial America*. New York: C. N. Potter, Inc., 1971.

Carson S., and Vick, A. W. *Hillbilly Cookin'*. Thorn Hill, Tenn.: Clinch Mountain Lookout, Inc., 1972.

Elverson, V. T., and McLanahan, M. A. *A Cooking Legacy*. New York: Walker & Co., 1975.

Frederick, J. G. *Long Island Seafood Cook Book*. New York: Dover Publications, 1971.

Kimball, Yeffe, and Anderson, Jean. *The Art of American Indian Cooking*. Garden City, N.Y.: Doubleday & Co., Inc., 1965.

Kluger, Marilyn. *The Wild Flavor*. New York: Coward, McCann & Geoghegan, Inc., 1970.

Leslie, Miss Eliza. *New Receipts for Cooking*. Philadelphia: Peterson, 1854.

Manyan, G. *The Country Seasons Cookbook*. New York: Crown Publishing Co., 1974.

Mirel, E. P. *Plum Crazy: A Book About Beach Plums*. New York: Crown Publishing Co., 1973.

Niethammer, Carolyn. *American Indian Food and Lore*. New York: Collier Books of Macmillan Co., 1974.

Rombauer, I. S., and Becker, M. R. *Joy of Cooking*. Indianapolis and New York: Bobbs-Merrill Co., 1931.

Russell, Helen Ross. *Foraging for Dinner*. New York: Nelson, 1975.

Stewart, Dr. A. M., and Kronoff, L. *Eating from the Wild*. New York: Ballantine Books, 1975.

Stobart, Tom. *Herbs, Spices and Flavorings*. New York: McGraw-Hill Book Co., 1970.

The Institute for Anquilliform Research and Mariculture. *The Eel Cookbook.* Bridgeport, Conn.: Univ. of Bridgeport Press, 1977.

Tinker, Alice, and Tinker, Sylvester. *Authenticated American Indian Recipes.* Pawhuska, Okla.: 1955.

Vigil, Priscilla. *Pueblo Indian Cookbook.* Sante Fe, N.M.: Museum of New Mexico Press, 1972.

Wallace, L. Haxworth. *Sea Food Cookery.* New York: M. Barrows & Co., Inc., 1944.

Wampanoag Cookery. Boston: The Children's Museum, 1974.

Whisler, Frances L. *Indian Cookin'.* Nowega Press, 1973.

Women's Alliance of the First Church of Deerfield, Mass. *The Pocumtuc Housewife: A Guide to Domestic Cookery.* Deerfield, Mass.: 1805.

Ethnobotany

Asch, David L., and Asch, Nancy B. "Chenopod as Cultigen: A Re-evaluation of Some Prehistoric Collections from Eastern North America." *Midcontinental Journal of Archaeology,* Vol. 2, No. 1 (1977), pp. 3 — 37.

Berglund, B., and Belsby, C. E. *Edible Wild Plants.* New York: Charles Scribner's Sons, 1977.

Coon, Nelson. *The Dictionary of Useful Plants.* Emmaus, Pa.: Rodale Press, 1974.

―――. *Using Wayside Plants.* New York: Hearthside Press, 1960.

Densmore, Frances. *How the Indians Use Wild Plants for Food, Medicine and Crafts.* New York: Dover Publications, 1974.

Fernald, M. L., and Kinsey, A. C. *Edible Wild Plants of Eastern North America,* rev. R. C. Rollins. New York: Harper & Row, 1958.

Hays, W., and Hays, R. V. *Foods the Indians Gave Us.* New York: Weathervane Books, 1973.

Hedrick, U. P. *Sturtevant's Edible Plants of the World.* New York: Dover Publications, 1972.

Lehner, Ernst, and Lehner, Johanna. *Folklore and Odysseys of Food and Medicinal Plants.* New York: Farrar, Straus & Giroux, 1973.

Mangelsdorf, Paul C. *Corn: Its Origin, Evolution and Improvement.* Cambridge, Mass.: The Belknap Press of Harvard Univ. Press, 1974.

Nathan, Joan. "An Indian Harvest Festival." Boston *Sunday Globe,* Nov. 28, 1976.

Saunders, Charles F. *Edible and Useful Wild Plants of the U.S. and Canada.* New York: Dover Publications, 1948.

Schultes, R. E., and Hill, A. F. *Plants & Human Affairs,* 2nd ed. Cambridge, Mass.: Botanical Museum of Harvard Univ., 1973.

Scully, Virginia. *A Treasury of American Indian Herbs.* New York: Crown Publishing Co., 1970.

Svoboda, Marie. *Plants That the American Indians Used.* Chicago: Chicago Natural History Museum, 1964.

Weatherwax, Paul. *Indian Corn in Old America.* New York: Macmillan Co., 1954.

Yanovsky, Elias. *Food Plants of the North American Indians.* U.S. Dept. of Agriculture, Miscellaneous Publication 237. Washington, D.C.: U.S. Government Printing Office, 1936.

Yarnell, Richard A. *Aboriginal Relationships Between Culture and Plant Life in the Upper Great Lakes Region,* Anthropological Papers. Ann Arbor, Mich: Univ. of Michigan Press, 1964.

Ethnology

Axtell, James. *The Native American People of the East.* West Haven, Conn.: Pendulum Press, Inc., 1973.

Curtin, J. C., and Hewitt, J.N.B. "Seneca Fiction, Legends and Myths." *Bureau of American Ethnology, 32nd Annual Report.* Washington, D.C.: U.S. Government Printing Office, 1910.

Curtis, Natalie. *The Indians' Book.* New York: Harper & Bros., 1907.

DeForest, John W. *History of the Indians of Connecticut from the Earliest Known Period to 1850.* Hartford, Conn.: Wm. Jas. Hamersley & the Connecticut Historical Society, 1851.

The Early Americans (film). Indianapolis: Shell Film Library, 1975.

Fenton, William N., ed. *Parker on the Iroquois.* Syracuse, N. Y.: Syracuse Univ. Press, 1968.

Fowler, Carol. *Daisy Hooee Nampeyo.* Minneapolis: Dillon Press, Inc., 1977.

Harrington, M. R. *The Indians of New Jersey: Dickon Among the Lenapes.* New Brunswick, N.J.: Rutgers Univ. Press, 1963.

Hertzberg, Hazel W. *The Great Tree and the Longhouse.* New York: Macmillan Co., 1966.

Howell, Kenneth T. *From the Pootatuck Indians to the Diggings at Kirby Brook Site in Washington, Connecticut.* American Indian Archaeological Institute Library, Washington, Conn.

Indians of the Eastern Seaboard. U.S. Dept. of the Interior, Bureau of Indian Affairs. Washington, D. C.: U.S. Government Printing Office, 1969.

Lamb, Trudie. Teacher and spokeswoman for American Indians for Development and for her people, the Schaghticokes.

Leland, Charles G. *The Algonquin Legends of New England or Myths and Folklore of the Micmac, Passamaquoddy and Penobscot Tribes.* Boston: Houghton Mifflin Co., 1884.

Logan, Adelphina. Teacher, artist, historian, lecturer, and leader for her people, the Onondagas.

MacNeish, Richard S. "The Origins of New World Civilization." *Scientific American,* Vol. 211, No. 5 (Nov. 1964), pp. 29–37.

———. "Ancient Mesoamerican Civilization." *Science,* Vol. 143, No. 3606 (Feb. 1964).

Marriott, A., and Rachlin, C. *American Indian Mythology.* New York: Thomas Y. Crowell Co., 1968.

Momaday, N. Scott. *The Way to Rainey Mountain:* Albuquerque, N.M.: Univ. of New Mexico Press, 1969.

More Than Bows and Arrows (film). Seattle, Wash.: Cinema Association, Inc., and the 13th Regional Corporation of Alaska Natives, 1978.

Rainey, Froelich G. "A Compilation of Historical Data Contributing to the Ethnography of Connecticut and Southern New England Indians." Ph.D. thesis, Yale Univ., 1933.

Richmond, David. Teacher, designer, and builder for his people, the Mohawks.

Sekatau, Eric, and Ella. Teachers, artists, and historians for their people, the Narragansetts.

Speck, Frank G. "Native Tribes and Dialects of Connecticut, A Mohegan-Pequot Diary." *Bureau of American Ethnology, 43rd Annual Report.* Washington, D.C.: U.S. Government Printing Office, 1925.

————. "Wawenock Myth Texts from Maine." *Bureau of American Ethnology, 43rd Annual Report,* Washington D.C.: U.S. Government Printing Office, 1925.

Swigart, Edmund K. *The Prehistory of the Indians of Western Connecticut.* Washington, Conn.: American Indian Archaeological Institute, 1974.

Warner, Frederic W. "Some Aspects of Connecticut Indian Culture History" (thesis). Ann Arbor, Mich.: Univ. Microfilms, 1971.

————. "The Foods of the Connecticut Indians." *Bulletin of the Archaeological Society of Connecticut, Inc.,* No. 37 (1972), pp. 27–47.

Washburn, Wilcomb. *The Indian in America.* New York: Harper & Row, 1975.

Guides and General Resources

Angier, Bradford. *Field Guide to Edible Wild Plants.* Harrisburg, P.: Stackpole Books, 1974.

————. *Feasting Free on Wild Edibles.* Harrisburg, Pa.: Stackpole Books, 1966.

Berglund, Berndt, and Bolsby, Clare E. *The Edible Wild.* Toronto: Pagurian Press, Ltd., 1971.

Brockman, F. C. *A Guide to Field Identification of Trees of North America.* Racine, Wisc.: Western Publishing Co., 1968.

Cobb, Boughton C. *A Field Guide to the Ferns.* Boston: Houghton Mifflin Co., 1956.

Crockett, James U. *Vegetables and Fruits.* New York: Time-Life Books, Inc., 1972.

Gibbons, Euell. *Stalking the Faraway Places.* New York: David McKay, 1973.

————. *Stalking the Healthful Herbs.* New York: David McKay, 1966.

————. *Stalking the Wild Asparagus.* New York: David McKay, 1962.

Hall, Alan. *The Wild Food Trail Guide,* New York: Holt, Rinehart & Winston, 1976.

Harris, Ben C. *Eat the Weeds.* New Canaan, Conn.: Keats Publishing Co., 1973.

————. *The Complete Herbal.* Barre, Mass.: Barre Publishing Co., 1972.

Leighton, Ann. *Early American Gardens.* Boston: Houghton Mifflin Co., 1970.

Lucas, Richard. *Common and Uncommon Uses of Herbs for Healthful Living.* New York: Arco Publishing Co., 1969.

Lust, John. *The Herb Book.* New York: Bantam Books, 1974.

McCleod, Dawn. *Herb Handbook.* North Hollywood, Calif.: Wilshire Publishing Co., 1968.

MacKenzie, Katherine. *Wild Flowers of the Northeast.* Plattsburg, N.Y.: Tundra Books, 1973.

Meyer, Joseph E. *The Herbalist.* New York: Crown Publishing Co., 1970. Facsimile reproduction of 1918 edition.

Peterson, Lee. *A Field Guide to the Edible Wild Plants of Eastern U.S.* Boston: Houghton Mifflin Co., 1978.

Peterson, Roger Tory, and McKenny, Margaret. *A Field Guide to Wildflowers.* Boston: Houghton Mifflin Co., 1968.

———, and Fisher, James. *Wild America.* Boston: Houghton Mifflin Co., 1955.

Thomas, Lewis. *The Lives of a Cell: Notes of a Biology Watcher.* New York: Viking Press, 1974.

Medicines and Mushrooms

Aikman, Lonnelle. *Nature's Healing Arts.* Washington, D.C.: National Geographic Society, 1977.

Elbaum, Katherine. "A Cultural and Medical Evaluation of Child Mummy from Ancón, Peru: Mummy Autopsy." Thesis, Univ. of Chicago, 1975.

Emmart, Emily W., trans. *The Badianus Manuscript: An Aztec Herbal of 1552.* Baltimore: Johns Hopkins Press, 1940.

Haard, R., and Haard, K. *Poisonous and Hallucinogenic Mushrooms.* Seattle, Wash.: Cloudburst Press, 1975.

———. *Foraging for Edible Wild Mushrooms.* Seattle, Wash.: Cloudburst Press, 1974.

Hand, W. M. *The House Surgeon and Physician.* Hartford, Conn.: S. Andrus & Son, 1847.

Harris, B. C. *Kitchen Medicines.* New York: Weathervane Books, 1968.

Krieger, L. C. *The Mushroom Handbook.* New York: Dover Publications, 1967.

Lehane, Brendan. *The Power of Plants.* New York: McGraw-Hill Book Co., 1977.

Miller, R. A., and Tatelman, D. *Magical Mushroom Handbook.* Seattle, Wash.: Homestead Book Co., 1977.

Millspaugh, Charles F. *American Medicinal Plants.* New York: Dover Publications, 1974. Facsimile reproduction of 1892 edition.

Ott, Jonathan. *Hallucinogenic Plants of North America.* Berkeley, Calif.: Wingbow Press, 1976.

Schultes, Richard Evans. *Hallucinogenic Plants.* Racine, Wis.: Western Publishing Co., Inc., 1976.

Tantaquidgeon, Gladys. *Folk Medicine of the Delaware and Related Algonkian Indians.* Harrisburg, Pa.: The Pennsylvania Historical and Museum Commission, 1972.

———. "Mohegan Medicinal Practices, Weatherlore and Superstition." *Bureau of American Ethnology, 43rd Annual Report.* Washington, D.C.: U.S. Government Printing Office, 1925.

Vogel, Virgil J. *American Indian Medicine.* Norman, Okla.: Univ. of Oklahoma Press, 1970.

Weiner, Michael A. *Earth Medicine—Earth Foods.* New York: Collier Books of Macmillan Co., 1972.

Principal Reference Resources

Bailey, Liberty Hyde; Zoe, Ethel; and the staff of the L. H. Bailey Hortorium. *Hortus Third*. New York: Cornell Univ. and Macmillan Co., 1976.

Driver, Harold E. *Indians of North America*. Chicago: Univ. of Chicago Press, 1969.

Fernald, Merritt L. *Gray's Manual of Botany*, 8th ed. New York: D. Van Nostrand Co., 1970.

Gleason, Henry A. *Britton and Brown Illustrated Flora of the Northeastern United States & Adjacent Canada*. New York: The New York Botanical Garden, 1952.

Hedrick, U. P. *Sturtevants's Edible Plants of the World*. New York: Dover Publications, 1972.

Millspaugh, D. F. *American Medicinal Plants*. New York: Dover Publications, 1974. Facsimile reproduction of 1892 edition.

Moeller, Roger W. "Seasonality and Settlement Patterns of Late Woodland Floral and Faunal Patterns in the Upper Delaware Valley." Ph.D. thesis, State Univ. of New York at Buffalo, 1975.

————, and Reid, John. *Archaeological Bibliography for Eastern North America*, ed. R. W. Moeller. Washington, Conn.: Eastern States Archaeological Federation and American Indian Archaeological Institute, 1977.

Parker, Sterling P., and Parker, Ruth. Botany identification, farm, and herbarium. Woodbury, Conn.

Seymour, F. S. *The Flora of New England*. Rutland, Vt.: C. E. Tuttle Co., 1969.

Watt, B. K., and Merrill, A. L. *Handbook of the Nutritional Contents of Foods*. New York: Dover Publications, 1975.

It is impossible to *catalog* all people, and yet it is the people, my richest
and most varied of resources, who make this book live:
  my grandmother and my mother, who have instilled in me
    the essence of nature, "to walk in harmony with all living things";
  my children — and for the sake of children;
  the native peoples from various tribal backgrounds who share in
    our research and progress at the institute;
  the librarians and libraries who have nurtured me;
  the many sincere and interested people who have shared with me
    their special knowledge and talents,
    particularly Susan Payne and
    the staff, trustees, and volunteers of AIAI;
  the people at Random House —

    my gratitude!

BOTANICAL INDEX

Page numbers in italics
indicate illustrations

GENERAL INDEX

About the Author

BARRIE KAVASCH is the staff ethnobotany teacher at the American Indian Archaelogical Institute in Washington, Connecticut. In addition to her work on *Native Harvests* for the AIAI, she is also setting up their herbarium, which indexes the plants used by the Eastern Woodlands Indians. She lives with her husband and two children in Bridgewater, Connecticut.

A Note on the Type

The text of this book was set in the film version of Weiss, a typeface originally cut in metal for the Bauer Foundry in Germany. Emil Rudolf Weiss created the first designs for this face in 1928. In 1966 the face was transferred to film for typositor setting, and was subsequently converted to keyboard photocomposition. Although essentially "old style" in character, the small serifs lend this face a contemporary elegance.

The text type was composed on the VIP photo-typesetting system by The Clarinda Company, Clarinda, Iowa. The book was printed and bound by the R. R. Donnelley Company, Crawfordsville, Indiana. Production and manufacturing were directed by Connie Mellon. The book was designed by Elissa Ichiyasu.